GODDESS INSPIRED

The Collected Writings

By

Raymond Pattison

(Ex-monk Paramhansa Ganesh Giri)

Copyright © 2022 Author *Raymond Pattison*

ISBN 9780473649449

All rights reserved.

CONTENTS

Preface

Chapter 1. **How to be Happy?**   Pg. 1

Chapter 2. ***Mantras, Kundalini, Shakti***   Pg. 48

Chapter 3. **Goddess Inspired spirituality**   Pg. 100

Chapter 4. The *Gunas* **–what is happening?**   Pg.145

Chapter 5. **Divine Grace!**   Pg.164

Chapter 6. **"Statements" or Aphorisms**   Pg. 217

Chapter 7. **Spirituality and mental wellness**   Pg. 241

Chapter 8. ***Life and the Universe***   Pg. 285

Chapter 9. **Practical Enlightenment**   Pg. 307

Preface to Goddess Inspired

This book is a follow on from my previous books.

It collects most of the *Goddess Inspired* Teaching writings from those books, and adds more.

My first book covered in depth my journey to India and then my ten years in India as a monk. (1966-1976). *English-man, Beggar-man, Holy-Man.*

Following books are: *Om Divine Grace and Grace Divine Journey.* Autobiographical plus teaching content.

I write to teach.

Life is a teaching in its journey.

I write for the purpose of providing information, teaching and reflection, with the purpose of engendering Enlightenment.

I was born in London 1947 and became a monk in India in 1966.

I returned to England in 1976 and then became a mental health practitioner.

I started a family life after moving to New Zealand, and I spent more than 10 years in clinical teaching or education roles. Hence my predilection for teaching!

My books focus on my spiritual/psychological experience.

It's all about Divine Grace for me!

I sincerely hope not to present from an ego or lower self-perspective. My Deity is not God or Higher Power, but the Goddess in the forms I became devotionally focused on in India. This Goddess is represented, (in plural), by Durga, Kali, Lakshmi and Sarasvati. (All One but separate just like us!).

As well as Tara, who is prominent in Tibetan Buddhism.

Just to clarify, I write about Enlightenment in terms of what we can all be, and in fact what we all are all in our Truth. Accepting ones Divinity is part of the journey, and this is not to denigrate religions or philosophies of Duality. I still maintain both a non-dual approach and a devotional one. Religion may however forcefully want to us to bow down before *their* gods, higher powers, saviours and avatars. I myself have found benefit in many religions through considerable active participation, whilst avoiding the fundamentalists. I add those resources to the list of what helped.

    I am Multi-Faith!

    I am "multi-modal". (Accepting scientific, psychiatric, and even atheistic viewpoints).

Can I do this? Currently free-thinking is still legal where I live, and long may this state of affairs continue!

Underpinning all of the journey therefore lies my years of practice and experience, and my intention to leave these writings as a resource for whoever finds them useful. My bottom line is that I write for myself! (With a perspective that I believe it's my service to provide this). It is a directed endeavour, driven by my Goddess and the Divine Cosmic Consciousness. I am also grateful for my Guides and guides, and my Gurus and gurus.

The writings in all the books are teachings.

My spiritual journey now is present as my Goddess Inspired writings.

It's not really a battle of opposites because in my spiritual philosophy both good and evil are elements of a spectrum. That spectrum is Divine Cosmic Consciousness of which we are all part, and therefore all participants in a learning experience. Our ego-based personality is also part of the Cosmic Divinity.

I have no time or place to consider an old man with a long white beard, sitting up in the clouds damning all those who don't do exactly as they're told! My God is Goddess. I have though a devotional mode that I picked up in India, but I don't think it necessarily is part of Hinduism only.

Goddess Inspired

It's universal, as the Goddess exists in all religions and cultures, and is the presentation in form of the formless Deity, who also provides life throughout consciousness, inner and outer space and the Cosmos.

As for health in its entirety and even life and its entirety, I call it: *Life and the Universe.*

I use this term to talk about life in general when I am trying to indicate spiritual and mundane matters or contrast the transcendental with what is not transcendental. (All at the same time).

I have now defined for myself the words R*ealization and Enlightenment*, because my Goddess is a practical power. She/he/it is the *Shakti or* energy of life on earth as we know it

Therefore, if we are to have any higher state of being both spiritually, and in the world as both human and divine, then we need to become:

> *Practically Enlightened*

> *Realistically Realized*

Some of the here material comes from quite different angles. (Its all really Goddess inspired though!). Feel free to delve into any parts or topics herein, and I do hope something is of interest. *Spacing is generous to allow "dipping in and out".*

Nothing is in any scientific order - it's just logical. Logical to me

Chapter 1
How to be happy

Happiness and "*Truth-Knowledge-Bliss*"

Why do we want to be happy? Does everyone want to be happy? Such questions seem to remain unanswered for ever. Nobody can hope to fully and scientifically analyse the state of mental happiness, nor explain easily why it is so important to us. What we can do however is to sidestep the theorising and practice of trying to define the intangible, and look at our wants in a realistic manner. We can and should get the most out of our lives, but not necessarily by any particular attainment. It seems a fallacy that success and happiness, (call it what you will), is to be *achieved,* if we believe that a state of perfection is no further than our true innermost self. Yet we do not see, except or recognise it, (this natural innermost self), easily. Why?

If we are really perfected souls, why then are we very imperfect? What can be more perfect in so many ways than the amazing facts of human life and the world and cosmos around us? So brilliantly designed and conceived and yet seen as so flawed in so many respects!

To answer our questions and realise a truth that is already there, we have to seek guidance usually. It is as if we are blind, and yet with help can reach a place where our eyes will be opened and we will see the truth of what has been described to us. In some ways it does not matter who guides us really or which path we take, as in time we will the probably find our own way. It is a matter of making the journey to start with, setting out and having a desire to be in a different, illuminated state of self-knowledge.

The word *self-knowledge* is a useful term to describe or mean the state that a seeker of happiness should attain. This ties in with an interest in a chosen spiritual philosophy that can be used as the core of the search to achieve and understand intellectual and spiritual goals. One such path or philosophy that we can draw on as a particular source for inspiration is *Vedanta*. (There are lots of books on this topic). In the eyes of the Western world, Vedanta seems to be part of Hindu philosophy, albeit at the extreme end of the scale, as it seems to present a somewhat strictly monotheistic view. (And be monastically inclined). It can be seen however as a universal expression of spiritual truths. In Vedanta the "apparent" world is *Maya*. We could say "unreal", although in slang that means "fantastic". We actually mean false or fake, in comparison to the essential Divine nature of the universe, which is *Anirvachaniya,* or a reality which "words and thoughts cannot reach".

How real is the body? It dies and then does not exist. How real is a dream? It ends and then does not exist. Where then one might ask has the real world been hidden? When we dream, we exist within a world that is very real to us at that moment, and the outside world is blocked out by sleeping mental and physical faculties. Life still exists, not really as a hidden world at all, as we know that the world around us goes on even when we sleep. We know this however by intellectual knowledge, not necessarily by any direct awareness that functions during our sleep. When we wake up from a weird dream, we know that the strange people and places we experienced were false reality. Yet we still feel a chill and awaking has not distanced us completely from our imaginings or dreaming.

If we walk out in the dark and see in the gloom something lying on the path in front of us we hesitate. Is it a snake? It may be just a piece of thick rope which appears in the gloom to be a snake. We are momentarily frightened until our eyes adjust to the object and we laugh inside at our silliness. In the murkiness of our minds, we erroneously perceive the world about us to be something other than it really is. When we are very young, we believed that the height of affluence, (when I was in England), was to possess a bag of sweets or a posh doll, a new cricket bat or a modern bicycle. Adults may laugh at childish naiveté yet see nothing about their own desires for a turbo model car or the latest in lounge furniture. No doubt someone in the heavens is looking down with amusement on the childish fantasies of fully grown adults, and yet we take ourselves seriously whether as children or senior citizens. All our games are usually played as real, and we do not want to be put down as daydreamers. Not until perhaps our last days when, as we know, there are quite a few conversions to some religion or philosophy on the deathbed. When we are about to depart this mortal world our prowess in chess or in sports, or on the stock exchange becomes a non-entity. People can remember us for our achievements when we are gone, but do we actually get to enjoy adulation as if we were alive and there?

Where is then the way to real happiness? Do we avoid the world completely because it is like passing dream? We cannot usually spend the whole time in trance, nor even alcoholic stupor or drugged euphoria. The reality of our continuous dream of life impinges upon our consciousness to a greater or lesser extent, whether we choose or not. We are bound by our bodies, upbringing and personal environment to live out our lives as long as we live. There is no simple escapist route that avoids the facts of life and death. Happiness then it anywhere and must live within our own experience, if it lies anywhere, or if it exists at all even.

Perhaps before we start spending any more of our time on the pursuit of happiness we should consider whether or not we are really wasting our efforts. We know, due to universal experience, that some states have an utter inner peace and tranquillity, and do exist even when we are in deep sleep. We can experience deep and profound rest from our problems and woes, and we know this because when we are awake, we say to ourselves that we had a wonderfully refreshing rest. If we are in pain and receive some injection that works, we can go into the state bordering on euphoria because of the effect of the drug, and also the release from an immediate and urgent physical pain. It's such a relief. On a more mundane level we might jump for joy when after days or weeks of some hassle or problem, and then we have a breakthrough or a change of luck perhaps. Note that often the arousal of happiness is almost dependent on some previous misery, tiredness or trouble. Happiness is achievable but may also be transient and the result of having an opposing unhappy time!

True happiness is not something achieved by a change of our mood in reference to our surroundings. True happiness is a natural state, unaffected by a good or bad luck, by tiredness, sleep, or by our pain or euphoria. True happiness is not even happiness at all, it is something else described in other words. Unfortunately we do not seem to have very suitable word or words in English language that properly refers to this state of being - that is not the result of external or mental influences. There is however in Sanskrit a very interesting phrase - *Sat, Chit, Ananda.* This phrase describes the state which is the very innermost nature of all life on earth and elsewhere. Sat means the Truth. Chit means Consciousness, and Ananda means Bliss. This is the description of the unchangeable inner soul, as well is that for the Divine cosmic presence. Truth-Knowledge-Bliss.

The way to our inner self is by negating or removing all the fluctuating and transient and moods that range from abject misery to wild euphoria. To do this we need some mechanism by which we can purify or still the fluctuating mental waves that wash hither and thither within our skull, like water in a bathtub. Note that we may not be able to subtract much from our thought patterns. We cannot just dump our mental processes, because there is no way of just removing them - except by dying, and there is nowhere else to put them. We do not need an extractor mechanism, we need something that will calm the turbulent emotions of grief and anger, elation and confusion, and allow the mind to become calm clear lake in which we can experience the reflected joy of our inner soul, and the Sat, Chit, Ananda of the Divine.

What is?

Vedanta: Means literally end of the *Vedas* and is a part of the vastness of Hindu philosophy. Vedanta however, on the surface, seems to oppose the Vedic and Hindu religion in a major way and on major points, and separates away from the concept of worshipping many gods or performing rituals. God is one transcendental state, without specifically denying the value and purpose of a personal god. It does critically analyse Vedic sacrifice and worship of the various deities, and even penance of the yogis. Vedanta seeks to clear away the clutter of ritual, and point to the discovery of the inner soul, the *Atman*, which is one with the cosmic soul, *Brahman*. Vedanta is not the pathway of devotion to a Personal God. It is a way of being already perfected souls in oneness with the whole of creation. It may be hard to swallow, that we ourselves are God, as the Atman is the same substance as Brahman. The Vedantic mantra is *Tat Twam Asmi* – That I Am. Or the mantra, *Soham* – I am that (Brahma), meditated on with the inhalations and exhalations of breath. I am Brahman, Cosmic Consciousness

Kundalini: Otherwise known as the serpent power, which is considered to be like a coiled snake of energy at the base of the spine. It can be coiled there in a dormant state and when awakened the energy or *Shakti* arises in a sinuous movement through the centre of the spine to the crown of the head. Along the way are centres of energy called *chakras* and each one of those chakras has specific and particular attributes.

Shakti: Considered to be the universal energy or Goddess energy - the creation force of the divine being. In this sense the masculine aspect of divine being is seen as a transcendental power which is beyond form and shape, and the female aspect is seen as the external creation. When practitioners worship the Shakti or Goddess form, they can worship the divine being as the world, the universe, or creation.

Mantra: is a Sanskrit word. The first part of the word means "constant thinking of" The second part of the word means "that by which one is protected."

So, by the conscience thinking of a certain word one is "protected', where the word protection has a wider connotation in spiritual terms, as being a means to a degree of perfection or S*iddhi.*

The part "*Man*" means literally to think and the word "*Tra*" means literally to protect or free.

The repetition or use of a mantra is considered to be enabling of a range of outcomes, from enlightenment down to the acquisition of wealth and pleasure.

The repetition of a mantra is called *Japa*. In Hinduism it is said in Scriptures that in this age, the Dark Age, (*Kali Yuga*), that the repetition of certain mantras is the easiest way to obtain enlightenment. However, there may not seem to be much science or evidence associated with such a view.

Chakra: In Sanskrit, chakra translates into "wheel". These "wheels" can be thought of as vortexes that both receive and radiate energy. There are seven major energy centres or chakras, in the human body.

They run from the base of the spine to the crown of the head. Emotions, physical health, and mental clarity affect how well each chakra can filter energy. This in turn dictates how pure the energy is that's emitted from different regions of the body.

Calming the mind

The Indian sages used a method called yoga, (meaning to yoke), and meditated on a light in the heart or used a hypnotic mantra. Mantra is a word or sound which is supposed to have real and direct junction with its sacred meaning. In all religions we find that there is some symbol or word usage that is used for the purpose of concentrating the mind, channelling it towards Divinity. Verbal formulae however is used also in witchcraft, primitive ritual and even the repetitive lines that we used to get as children in school when we got detention. It is not so much a question of the word sound or sentence itself, but rather the repetition that is intended to concentrate the mind.

Repetition is a rather negative way to go about achieving some degree of one pointed concentration, as it then becomes a matter of blocking thoughts. When we study or watch a good film or some sport, we have focused the mind and blocked the world and its problems outside. When we come out of the film into the cold night air, for all the distraction that the film engendered we return to the same world.

That is not to say that the value of mantra as repetitive practice is a negative means to achieving either mental tranquillity or happiness. The point is that the real permanent and changed happiness, (with a capital H), is something else - a separate entity. It is a natural achievable entity but unfortunately sometimes seems to lie at the heart of a maze. Just as a person with a map can find a route through a strange city, so if we are equipped with a map of the workings and ways of the subtle mental forces behind a world existence, we can plot our way to the heart of reality. We need to know what the mind is, what it does and how it functions. We need to know the effect of our mind on our lives, our personalities, and most importantly on happiness. We need to know how other minds affect ours, and understand national minds, and culture.

If the information that we need for our map is beginning to sound a bit complex don't worry. Even in a big city like London if we wish to reach the centre we only need to approach from one direction, as we only need one route in order to reach a goal. Similarly, if we wish to weave our way through the minds maze and hit the centre, we only need some fairly simple instructions of and knowledge of what we are likely to encounter on the way - the landmarks as it were.

It is easier if you have a space in which to think and reflect in peace and quiet. You therefore set aside time for your purpose in this matter, leaving family friends and business to wait a while, making the spiritual journey a very important part of your life. Unlike money in the bank this is practice that you can take with you to the beyond, so, sit on your own and reflect or meditate, whether it be everyday week or month. Without these recharging interludes, our human spiritual batteries run flat, and sometimes we even become incapable of resolving simple ordinary life conflicts, let alone deep meaning full ones. Taking out your own time and space is not antisocial; it allows you to develop into a better person all round.

Many perceive that withdrawal from social activities is only negative, but "non-activities" are not destructive. It is the very nature of the world that it throws up to each individual "waiting periods". It is a natural protective phenomenon even when nothing seems to be happening and even if we feel frustrated, agitated, or bored when we cannot be getting on with something. If we can imitate nature's own method, and create our own quite uneventful periods, we control better our destiny and future. (Instead of being like a leaf that is blown hither and thither by events and people around us). There are a variety of phenomena that are sometimes placed upon us by circumstance, and free seemingly empty time may not be an easily acceptable space, simply because of how we may perceive it.

It is also something of a shock that having sat down, having cleared a space, and started meditating, that agitation, boredom etc. may arise and dominate the mind. This meditative space can be a wonderful and necessary refuge but may also stir a variety of unwelcome thoughts that had not been in the plan. This may be why we don't hear much public eulogy about the benefit of meditation, because it is a common experience that sitting down even to 5 or 10 minutes in absolute stillness can be akin to herding cats! The mind is a wild untamed creature for many, which leads rather than is lead. When you decide to do something about this and have a disciplined state of affairs, the mind (or perhaps rather the ego), can become most upset and tries to resist attempts at any form of mental introspection. Meditation can be difficult and even "depressing" - that is just the first obstacle!

To overcome the fickle mind is not easy and it may seem impossible to get to a state of perfect yoga. A perfect yogi is not one who can sit in a cave motionless in months at a time. If one controls his or her mental environment wherever that may be, the setting is not so important. However, environment can play a large part in any yogic practice as suitable surroundings, access to guides, and spiritual information, may help aid the mental processes. We can only do so much and only afford so much of our time getting into mental shape, but we cannot mend perfectly a pot that is broken and from which there are a few pieces permanently missing. We do what we can in this respect, just like bringing an older car up to a state of roadworthiness by fine tuning and renovation.

When we practice yoga for our physical well-being it is called *hattha yoga*. This is a system of exercise, not just to make a fit and healthy body, but to assist in purifying our mind. Purification of the body means that even the subtle and microscopic parts of the nervous system are cleansed, paving the way for higher mental-based exercises. Such exercises lead then from action (*Kriya)* yoga to *Raja* (Kingly) yoga path, where we move on then to meditation via specific exercises and perhaps use of mantras. Sounds or words associated with inward spiritual states require time to practice achieving perfection or attainment, (siddhi), in sufficient depth. This may seem difficult as most of us cannot aspire to the heights of ascetics who live in caves and meditate all their waking hours. However, mantra meditation, once set into solid rhythm and practice, can be made into an effortless aspect, as then it can be done whilst doing other activities at any time. We need something that doesn't need us to dip into our precious time and enables us to boost mood to something better than bearable. We need to be able to transcend our daily problems at times without having to put ourselves into a trance like state of mind.

Advaita Vedanta, or "without duality" is not the pathway of devotion to a Personal God. The very form or substance of life *is* Sat-Chit-Ananda, or Existence-Consciousness- Bliss. All that Vedanta treatises teach can seem a far cry from the world of organised religion, messiahs, bishops and infallible preachers. Advaita Vedanta is almost a "godless" philosophy, almost an atheistic philosophy in some ways. It is a way to realisation as understanding of us and the world as it really is, free from any supernatural power or need for religious belief. Broadly speaking it is not even a Hindu only philosophy, as it is a universal creed that owes allegiance to no religious persuasion.

Many books have been written about the subject in depth, and all the Vedanta scriptures have been the subject of exhaustive and numerous commentaries by a variety of learned scholars, both Eastern and Western, both ancient and present. You can obtain enough books and information about the subject to last you a lifetime's reading. The problem though, is the application of this concept of being God, or even Godlike, or even of the same substance as God. It is difficult especially when we are tied up with work, marriage and business. When we are tied up with the world of Maya (illusory nature), it can be difficult to really believe that we as individuals are nothing but pure consciousness which has taken various transient human forms within this mire of externalised experience.

When we struggle with depression or addictions or other issues is can seem "mission impossible" to even get a foothold in the spiritual dimension.

To repeat the mantra *Soham* we are saying "I am identical with all the pervasive external and internal life force", and we are practising a philosophy that says don't identify yourself with body or mind, or with your role in the day ahead. It's a simple deep breathing, with mantra in tune with the essence of self, which will help you to float through the day in serenity. It is useful to wake up 5 to 10 minutes before you need to do anything and use that short space of time in vital introspection. You need to make your day goes smoothly, so give yourself time to reflect, and try to visualise the individual power of being merged into the big wide Universe. Breathe Soham to surrender your day into the Divine aspect of the forces which control the circumstances you are to encounter. (You cannot avoid some trying circumstances ahead of you, although you plan or program to do this and try to have a large say in the proceedings). Worrying will not necessarily change things for the better, but learning to relax and be meditative allows you to flow with events that you're unable to control, and you may find yourself doing things more easily and more smoothly than you've even planned! A clear mind is always beneficial in any circumstance, and will often help you to come up with the right answer to problems.

The external world - the natural world - can be called seen as energy or Shakti, which is the goddess or feminine form of Creation. Creation as in contrast to the transcendental form of "masculine" energy, but it doesn't have to be seen as separate, nor Atman as separate from Shakti. Taking this further all the processes of life can be seen as being part and parcel of our soul work, and we can then also look at meditating a Trinity of Brahman, Shakti, and Atman. The knowledge of our world, and being able to manage work, money and relationships will also enable us to have a stronger hold on spiritual practice. When we are moving more towards or "expanding" our practice to overtly manage our world for both material and spiritual benefit, we are practicing *Tantra*, as Tantra means "to expand out". (Nothing to do with sex!).

Work for most of us is a perfectly natural function as we are guided by a natural qualities and abilities into doing tasks for which we are most suited. It may seem that we often find ourselves doing something we neither wish to do nor are suited to do, but if we can allow our natural destiny and intrinsic divine nature to predominate, we can move into different spaces of allowing ourselves to find our natural work position. Seen in this light a soldier who fights because he born a warrior type personality, is simply fulfilling his destiny, even though his work may involve killing other humans! He is complying with a subtle set of universal laws that govern all out work.

Such ideas may not appeal to a pacifist and those who seek to stop war. A lot of us say we believe in an ideally peaceful world. The historical reality however is that this has not happened and is not happening tomorrow. An individual can change society to a degree, but the essential nature of humankind, (and the universe), cannot be changed. Scientists working on genes may say that in theory we could build a non-violent selfless person in the future. However, in reality we will probably want to build something that is more akin to a Hollywood film star, rather than seeking tolerance and love for all! What we can do as individuals and collectively is develop our self-awareness and internal happiness to a point where the problems of our own making and our own human nature can be *transcended or accepted* as part of our divine journey.

The Calmed Mind

When there is searching or seeking the journey continues. At some stage you want to be more than a searcher - and be one who has *arrived.* When you reach the right place, you don't need to go further. Enlightenment is occurring at the same time as the journey is ceasing, when all diversion and digression, and the need to block the mind stops. Simply being is a present and natural state, inherent and always active. A position where all the spiritual, religious, yogic, psychiatric, and personal growth trips and efforts are cleared. Like a breakthrough of the sun. Even if all of our life, (or lives), may seem to have no real meaning, when achieving this place, one will become truly grateful, and see all that has gone before as the work of the Divine through the human. We don't need to become enmeshed in our own beliefs or practices from this perspective, as at the end of the day we don't need the path anymore, nor the guru, the teacher, or even a defined God. The purest elevated form of existence flows into a native state of spiritual enlightenment otherwise experienced as Existence, Knowledge, Bliss, or Sat-Chit-Ananda. This position has been known and written about over thousands of years from the time of the ancient sages and is prior to most known established religions. Nearer in history if we look closely it is expounded upon eloquently by all religions, albeit it in a variety of words, expressions and philosophy.

There are endless permutations of developed codes of religious practice, rituals and rules that are supposed to bestrew some benefit, giving a good credit rating towards the heavenly rewards. Sometimes this leads to some rejection of human natural activity such as the seeking of sex or wealth, even though the very acceptance of the human nature is also connected with Divine awareness. (From a Tantric perspective). In the here and now, the individual who is struggling to spiritually succeed seeks a way, which is lit up by the presence and involvement of teachers, sages or *gurus*. The true guru is the Sat (True) teacher. "*Gu*" means to "break through", while "*Ru*" means "darkness". You chose or ask for guidance on your journey, and seek it from a human teacher form, (even if not still alive). This imparter of the teaching or dispeller of darkness may just subtly project Shakti, enabling achievement of the required goal. For the spiritual seeker the guru is a grace that appears to the degree that the seeker has prepared to surrender to the guidance. It is a spark of recognition that jumps the gap between the teacher and the follower or disciple to light up the inner fires.

This following of the teacher or the guru is also part of a way, which is not about following one's basic desires, but about dealing with one's basic desires. Getting past what is binding. The characteristic behaviour or activity of an enlightened being can seem at times very ordinary or normal: A human who behaves as a human. But the path set down by the teacher endlessly addresses the problem of trying to get past or out of the human predicament, and the greed, hate, and desires that afflict us. It is then about accepting human nature and working with one's problems, continuing to practice, and not giving up on the journey in spite of lapses or even relapses from the path. There is no forceful asceticism or strident moral posturing, nor religious crusading. It is then the way of accepting the **Grace** and energy of the enlightened being and simply allowing that to promote one's own spiritual state until all the searching and seeking fall away.

Looking for the Tiger

No tigers here!

I left India after ten continuous years of living there. I had not been home at all in the period and had not contacted my parents or anyone outside India. Until that is I wrote to my parents in London, and as a result received a ticket to fly Bombay to London. I returned home in 1976 having left London in 1965 at the tender age of seventeen. (Went on the overland trail as a "Hippy" beatnik, smoked lots of "hashish" and spent a year getting to India. I had no income at all!)

(See my book about this period: *English-Man, Beggar-Man, Holy-Man*).

My years in India were spent as a *sadhu,* a Hindu holy man, a monk, and travelling yogi. I spent several years in several different places in India. I had a first guru that I ran away from after four years never to make contact again. Later after seven years in India I met *Swami Muktananda* in a place called *Genesh Puri*, (literally - the town of Ganesh, an Indian God). I stayed ten months in that large ashram, where Swami Muktananda had large numbers of his overseas followers. Americans, British, Australian and others were flocking to become his disciples. I stayed and had my name changed to *Ganesh Giri,* a sannyasin, (renunciate), name. However, I never took any formal initiation into the holy orders and indeed was told that I was first and foremost an English man and would always be so. I never considered myself at the time, a full disciple of Swami Muktananda, in the mould of the rest of his Western and Indian flock. I preferred to hang around in the background and take things a bit more cautiously. I left his ashram because I wanted to see my inner guru as well as an outer one. I wanted self-realisation for myself within myself.

After all that was what Swami Muktananda taught – that the guru and the Divine was within.

I spent my last three years in India living in the backwoods of Gujarat State, in a hut, thinking about little in particular, and wondering what my role in life was. I had no books or reading material or wristwatch. I just spent days and months mulling over my experiences to date with all the guru's and yogis I had met in India. I came to the conclusion eventually that I had a different type of life to experience awaiting me in England, and that the time was not yet right to plunge into a lifetime of living in India as a recluse or sannyasin.

At the age of twenty-eight, this return to my starting point in London was a big shock to my parents.

As mentioned, I left home alone and in 1965. I was seventeen and had at that time being restless to wander off and explore the world. The flames of rebellion burned within me. Rebellion from society, from parents, from the straitjacket of convention. I was not alone - the 60s were a time of foment, with the new pop culture leading, as espoused by the life, (and music of course), by the likes of the Beatles and the Rolling Stones. It was a period delineated through the birth of a youthful revolution that was to overturn the cultural norms of society at that time. The anti-establishment new generation wanted to explore new dimensions of experience, to grow long hair, wear outrageous clothes, and to experience hitherto unexplored depths of the mind with cannabis and LSD.

Influenced by my own generation I ended up on the India trail - the overland trip to Kathmandu and Nepal. I preceded a mass migration by several years, as by the time Westerners were flocking to India to guru is in large numbers, I had been ensconced there for about five years

After ten plus months on the hippy trail I reached India. The culture, like a magnet sucked me in and did not, for a while, spit me out. During my ten years continuous stay in India I met a variety of gurus, yogis, holy men and holy women. I travelled the length of the country and at times my bed was bare concrete and my stomach was empty. Increasingly I was feted, garlanded and dined in splendour by prostrating devotees who revered all holy men, (as I had become). At the end of it all I returned to England, almost following a spur of the moment decision. I ceased overnight to speak and think and dream in Hindi. Similarly, my wraparound cloths became trousers and shirts, and I became a conventional working Englishman.

On return to England, I had little to say on the subject of my Hindu monk's life. It was a role with which I had completely identified during my stay in India, and now I was finished with it and wanted no more of it. I wanted to be the Englishman again and take on that role, but not now as a dropout hippy. I wanted to work, buy a car, drink in pubs, watch the "telly", and construct a social life for myself that was not in any way religious.

I decided on being a social worker but found that I was not wanted due to my lack of work experience. It was difficult explaining just how I passed my ten idle years in India. I found it hard once even to get a job cleaning down tables in a café! By chance or circumstances, I came to apply for a position as a student psychiatric nurse. In many ways I became the average man in the street, or the ordinary guy in the pub. I more or less forgot about my role in India to the extent even of feeling vaguely embarrassed by it all. I immigrated to New Zealand after three years and travelled around between working as a psychiatric nurse. I did think about my yoga occasionally and from time to time remembered my mantras - the sacred words that I had been initiated into in India. Occasionally I would have periods where my inner meditations would be quite profound, although externally I carried on my routine of whatever I was into that time. The spiritual side of me did pop up a few times externally. Eventually I began to think again of the spiritual aspects of my life, although I did nothing much about it until 1985. It was whilst living in Andorra that I wrote my book about my ten years in India. In 1987 I was back in New Zealand after a sojourn in various parts of Europe, (France, Monte Carlo Andorra and Spain as well as in Wales).

Then ten years had gone by in the West, in the materialistic net. I thought I was back at the beginning of a new phase that promised much more ahead. I had had ten years learning about mental illness, relationships, the way of the world, and sundry matters. I had also been lucky to have had the great fortune to experience life in some other fascinating countries and places. Now I add another thirty years plus on to this "saga". (With these writings, and perhaps more?)

The title of this part of the book: *No tigers here* - means what?

When I was a child in London I used to dream about tigers a lot, and think they were wandering outside the block of flats that I lived in. I used to read a lot of books about hunting man eating tigers and leopards and lions. After living in India, I came to believe that I'd lived there before, and that all my childhood processes had been regurgitating aspects of a previous life in India. I saw myself as having been a hunter of tigers, who then became a non-violent devotee of tigers. In dreams in India, I saw myself meeting a yogic sage outside a cave and being admonished and turned away from my hunting to become a respectful devotee of the tiger. That dream was about my previous birth: not the current one. I may have been part of the British Raj in India: possibly a collector or some official living upcountry. In India tigers were often a part of my life: certainly spiritually, as the tiger is considered to be the vehicle of the Goddess *Durga.* However, when I moved away from India I didn't think then about tigers for quite a few years. My life was not connected like it had been with India and tigers, and my worship of the Goddess. (Now I am very different and the tiger is a core part of my life).

Finding the Tiger

In 1989 I married and over the next 30 plus years I became a family man and remain so to this time of writing. (2022). I extended my career to a satisfactory position as a senior health professional educator within mental health. I studied and received further qualifications and worked within a variety of interesting areas. However, one key element for me over this time to the recent was my struggle to deal with a seemingly ingrained experience of *Dysthymic Depression*. (Chronic low-grade depression). I have also experienced some addictive type of behavioural issues (dependant mostly on the depression).

> *There is a huge paradox. Now I have got to a place where I feel that I am really engaged as a spiritual soul to the maximum depth that I*

could ever wish, and I have found my self-realisation and my perfection (siddhi) on the spiritual plane. Yet it has come to be connected integrally with my experience of struggle with mental health issues at times.

Interestingly I find that as I relate now to the personality that I left in India as the Hindu monk, I see that my time of ten years in India was probably about sitting in the same space where I am can sit now. (Without the need for a cave!). Also, I can look back at myself in India and make a diagnosis of depressive episodes, mostly related to the mild-to-moderate chronic depression that is called dysthymia.

I am fascinated now by this paradoxical connection of intense deep spiritual experience and equally intense depression and also significant anxiety at times.

This for me is: *Finding the Tiger.* The tiger is my soul animal - similar to a favourite animal but not quite! The tiger represents me as being a complete whole person. Powerful in that I have my spiritual plane again, but also powerful in that I am a complete human being. I am human with my experience of some of the depths of despair and depression whilst at the same time have become able to deal with and cope with this part of my life. This adds to my power. I have experienced common place reality for many: the human life which can be, "weak, disabled and dysfunctional", and I am happy about this because I don't see it as bad. However, I also can be a functional health professional, family man, and "healthy human". All this alongside the choice of continuing my practice of spiritual awareness. This is about finding the Tiger: the tiger memories that drove me when I was a child to go to India, and to head off to end up as a monk. This metaphor for life has driven me now to look at the issue of spirituality and religion, and also depression or other mental health/addiction issues in some depth.

Taming the Tiger

Not a popular path! (Spiritual endeavour). You may find few who are willing or interested in listening to your politics and religion. Your personal growth and spirituality may be in a similar vein. You then find you need to talk to specific people who are clearly interested or committed in some form of growth. Personally interested people are willing to discuss spiritual topics. However, when this topic is broached, it may be that interested parties will then talk about or even try to sell their particular brand of spirituality, which may well be connected with a specific religion. Even in company of spiritual practitioners we can find difficulties dealing with fixed rigid views, and even angrily hostile perspectives. This may be why many are put off even by the whole topic. It may seem like a can of worms.

On the whole most of society seems to be quite happy engaging in the material consumer world, except for when it bites back, and they find that suffering rather than enjoying becomes the experience. Then may arise desire for something else. The truly selfless person, the true soul seeker, does not want anything. There is a spiritual goal and transformation of purpose, but that is also selfless: it's not like a dog finding a bone and running off.

We find some of these painful experiences about life out as we go through our years. Being somewhat protected as children, we may seek again more security as we get a bit older. In our hearts we may want to develop and grow in a holistic spiritual manner and believe our path of spiritual growth will enable us to sit back in and be protected or safe. However we may find that there are dangers in exploring and trying to move forward on a spiritual path, even though we may hold "magical thoughts" about how "wonderful" it will all be! There is even research that shows evidence of spiritual endeavour increasing mental health problems like depression. Addictions, compulsions or other psychological snakes may rear their heads, almost as if the ego fears it's "death" and wants to strike back.

Conversely it may seem that if one does all this practice with no sense of reward or desire, the goal may seems like some kind of hollow empty state - wilderness or a desert. Without actually tasting the nectar, the bliss of the Supreme Divine Grace, it is easy to feel emptiness (especially if one has given up lots of habits). Hence we may live for a while only trusting and hoping, when we follow chosen teachings, or believe that a higher power or Divinity will "sort our lives out".

Religion can be based around desires to prosper, to flourish, to have a good place in society, or to get to heaven. We then will maintain belief and trust that God will help us to get all the things we want and help us to do the right things. The spiritual journey though, (and this is where the difference really sits), is about transcending all of this. About becoming selfless, transforming a humanness into "spiritualness – not saintliness". There is nothing wrong with being human wanting or achieving or seeking.

Human experience itself will show the way, for when a goal is reached, this can lead to dissatisfaction and a need to go deeper. The bliss of money, food and sex will never ultimately be a permanent satisfaction or consolation. Seeking on the higher levels is where we want to have some taste of the Divine Grace nectar. We want to overcome some of the pain, sadness or general feeling of malaise about the world. We might start to feel this spiritual centre more, especially as we dig deeper into the spiritual world, and start to overhaul our materialistic striving. Choice will always remain the individuals, and that choice will always be to go forwards or backwards or just stay in the same place.

Probably not many choose to follow the path of spirituality to its deepest depths, nor would many want to become priests, monks, recluses or swamis. That however is not necessarily all of the potential "advanced" options. True monastic status essentially is an inner one in these modern times. Monasticism is something that was representative of spiritual or religious leaning more commonly in older times. The modern world doesn't leave much space around us to pursue that option. We have to do a lot of it on the internal plane, by making our own Divine connections and meeting in spaces where like-minded people can gather to do this work, without necessarily wearing certain clothes or performing certain rituals.

The biggest obstacle of all, is the part of us that doesn't want to die, and yet gives us most grief, and that is our ego. That is, when we seek to move into higher levels or planes the ego feels a threat, and may well set up its own conflicts and diversions to distract us for a long time. It is like a cat being removed from the warm fire to be put out into the cold – total reluctance! The human choice of life is to be very comfortable thank you very much. The way of the renunciate is not universally, commonly, or popularly cherished.

Our guides

There seems to be a series of doubts to do with how our spiritual or religious leaders have presented themselves. There are many sources of some hard questioning about gurus and spiritual teachers, now that we have the worldwide spread of the Internet. We can delve into subtle, (and not so subtle), truths about those who practice a religious or spiritual life, in the public domain. There are questions about why many of such persons have not been able to achieve what may be considered to be, a balance, a harmony, or even sanity. Was there something intrinsically wrong with the person to start with, or did some "pollution" occur? Is it an ego somehow being bolstered up by spiritual or religious kudos and acclaim? Even looking at older historical records of activities of great religious leaders, there have at times been things that are prompts for disgust. The modern media will spread gleefully, gory or outrageous accounts of the doings of major charismatic religious figureheads, be they of any religion. Christian pastors, Buddhist leaders and of course some really power crazed but charismatic leaders of brand-new sects, where even mass suicide has occurred. Totalitarian ministries, profligate sexual practices, or stupendous consumption of wealth is not uncommon. Where then is a serious seeker of truth to look, when seeking a path or guru?

There is instability engendered by building on one's fears and doubts, even if they have some truth, and this process should have some prominent ground in the seriously seeking enquiring mind. In all life it is best to avoid naive mistakes and blatant errors of judgement. There is also a need for some critical judgement, as to whether normal human behaviour is realistic for those with an expression of higher spiritual endeavour. Our journey is similar to a major journey or an expedition overseas. To go travelling with any company or guide, some enquiry and checks are needed. Find out about where you are going or why you want to go. Spiritual needs can be at times overwhelming and propel a person directly into acting rather than thinking.

So it is probably not realistic to expect that the spiritual enlightened are all going to be fully virtuous models of society, and paragons of morals, or even nice people! It would be nice to think so, but the reality is that anyone even at the higher levels, will still be inhabiting a human body. If they are dead and long gone: E.G. Jesus or Buddha; then we are not going to get much "dirt" on them, which makes things easier. However, we may not benefit from shunning alive teachers of any description, and in fact a lot of our life is built around having teachers, so we can reap benefit in our learning journeys. We need our many guides, and as long as we realise what we are using those guides for and avoid being sucked into some game. It is probably realistic to think that any guide that espouses higher level philosophy or spiritual practice, is only going to be relatively free of behavioural problems, addictions and negative personality traits. We do know that many in the world follow religious teachers who exhort their followers to go out and kill others, and it doesn't seem to put those followers off in the slightest. I would not see such persons as being teachers of any degree of spirituality. Religious teachers they may be, but then religion has always been associated with acts of aggression!

It seems that at some stage of the spiritual journey a conscious stock taking has to be done of all the subtle and more obvious mental, physical and emotional tendencies. Those which seem reasonably benign, (and yet set in concrete), may even be left unchanged as the spiritual goal is not human perfection, in spite of what organised religion may try to thrust upon people. The individual may choose a relatively saintly path, with or without outward display. On the other hand, the individual may simply take an, I don't care, attitude with regard to how the world responds. The spiritual journey is not about walking through a desert wilderness. There are times when there can be many temptations, as benefits may accrue from being on this journey, and temptations may be just what the ego is putting in our way to knock us back a bit.

Only at the higher stages of divine practice, and at the end of the journey does the light of perfection shine clearly.

The True Guru

"My cat is enlightened so why can't I be? Why do I still need a guru"?

Cats have it all sussed. Laze around all day in the house. No chores, no responsibilities and yet they are independent and free as they want to be. They stay out as late as they like, come and go when they please, and plenty of them have trained their owners as well, with regards to feeding times and other requirements. They are the gurus of the animal world certainly, and at times the envy of humans.

So, what's the need then to be taught better "tricks"? Why can't we just learn from nature and the people around us? Isn't a baby the best example of someone experiencing an inherently blissful natural state? Is certainly there are no shortages of learning experience on a day-to-day basis, (if we choose to accept them as such). There are people all around from whom we can learn at all times. We can also learn from our own mistakes, and from those of others. If we pursue a higher goal then there are plenty of books, and exercises to be practised, or philosophies to be pursued. In time it is quite logical, that, from the learning an individual could get a good idea of what Enlightenment, *Nirvana*, or *Moksha* is all about, and even find out how to get on the path towards such goals. (Nirvana, or Moksha are words used by Hindus or Buddhists and are Sanskrit words that describe a state of release from the cycle of birth and death, pleasure and pain).

The spiritual journey is open to anyone at any time. There are no rules which say you must have a guide, a teacher or a guru. Rather there is an understanding that all focused and energetic efforts on the spiritual journey will bring good rewards. In fact, it is logical that if you have gleaned good solid information yourself you will get better results than if you accept willy-nilly someone professed guidance, which may lead you into a mess. I am reluctant to follow recipes when cooking, as I much prefer the results, and taste, which I get from little judicious experimenting myself. The satisfaction of my own recipe gives me much more than that achieved using a textbook guide. However, in some areas, such as baking in my case, I always use a recipe!

Having a guru for the spiritual journey may even be dangerous, unless you are prepared for the acceptance of, and then proper use of, such a teacher. It's like buying a serious, expensive supercar when you are a learner driver, or when you only do a bit of city shopping by car. Or do you plan to run a Rolls-Royce if you are employed on the "lower socio-economic scale" (i.e. poor)? Real gurus are not to be trifled with; they are for those who are willing to accept some painful truths. Also, casual acceptance of any teacher may be a gateway for further neurotic anguish rather than peace and bliss. The word guru means "one who leads from darkness to light". A guru must be already in the light to be able to reach out and help others to attain the same illumination. A guru can only affect others to the degree of that guru's own achievement.

What benefits then are to be gained by the following of an enlightened being? That teacher, that guru, may not even be alive in a physical sense. As long as the teaching remains with some system or path to be followed, then the aspirant on the spiritual journey can benefit in proportion to the efforts made. The difference with the living human guru is that, a dead teacher is not going to come along with a cane to administer a rap on the knuckles. By taking on a living teacher, one is opening up to immediate evaluation, to being given marks, as in exams, and to being critically examined. The teacher is not working to allow comfort in the student. The student is not working to remain static in knowledge.

The spiritual aspirant who uses a living guru, will submit the dross, the mundane, and the un-enlightened mentality for the guru's inspection. The guru prescribes the medicine and the aspirant then moves on to the next stage - whether to take the medicine or not. The spiritual journey as gleaned from books may be quite palatable, but what the living guru may require of you personally may be "too much". This is the very reason why the true guru is necessary. If you want the spiritual journey to proceed apace, you can't stay in your comfort zone!

It's moving out of the comfort zone that is very hard, that is difficult to achieve without guidance. It is being open to inspection and evaluation that can be very uncomfortable but can be so productive. This is where the guru can work to help the spiritual aspirant. When the guru is found by a careful, even choosy search, and when the guru is approached in the appropriate manner, then the guru becomes the means for rapid progress on the spiritual journey. It is quite possible to progress spiritually by one's own efforts, and there is nothing inappropriate about this. Using the benefits of an enlightened guide however is like taking the express train rather than the slow goods train that gets "bumped off" into numerous sidings.

The spiritual smorgasbord including the New Age, therapies, various sects, cults and new religions can be a temptation leading to endless side journeys, with the self-taught student ending up aimlessly sailing in a lake of spiritual hope, without getting to see the shore. A knowledgeable guru has the present time experience of spiritual peace, awareness, and bliss that comes with real practice. This knowledgeable awareness can be "transmitted" to a student by subtle means that are not easily understood by a novice. In Sanskrit the word for this transmission is *Shakti-Paat,* the bringing down of divine Shakti energy by the guru to help awaken the natural abilities of the student, so that here and now something more concrete can be experienced regarding the nature of the spiritual goal. In Hinduism and Buddhism this energy transference is known to awaken the "third eye", or to awaken the sleeping Kundalini serpent force up through the spine. The third eye is just one way station for the chakras or centres of energy. Other areas awakened are in the heart area, the spinal centre, and also another heart "space", that is directly connected to Divine Energy.

You can choose your cat to be your guru, indeed as you can choose any person as a teacher. However, if you wanted to learn to fly jumbo jet would you take lessons from a bus driver?

Chapter 2
Mantras, Kundalini, Shakti

There is a view that the chanting of mantras is a practice to help focus the mind.

However, this view is a very partial perspective.

A mantra of any power exists in a totally different dimension to the mind.

It is a syllable, word, and sound that relates to a particular state of consciousness that, whilst related to mind, (and body), emanates from a soul or spirit source.

For instance, to use the word Guru as a mantra, is to identify on a subtle plane with the role of the Guru, which is to lead from darkness to light, from ignorance to knowledge, (in a spiritual sense).

In simple terms Gu refers to darkness and Ru to light.

Combined with Om, which is the spiritual word for and sound of the Universe, the mantra then both identifies and takes the user from darkness to light, or to the universe centre.

The practitioner, (who repeats or chants the mantra), becomes immersed in a sense of being at the centre of all life and light. Thus, to meditate with this mantra, the best effect occurs with visualisation of journeying out of the body, beyond the city, the country, the solar system, the galaxy, and so forth. (A continuation would be that of ascending to the universe Centre).

Then what happens?

Samadhi

This position at or within the Centre is the deepest form of meditation, (called Samadhi), with regard to external meditation on this aspect of the Divine.

However, to think that the human consciousness then cannot exist is not quite correct.

For instance in deep sleep it seems that the individual does not exist, yet on awakening all awareness comes back again.

In a further development of the Samadhi state the seeker needs then to find the Centre within the human "heart", (not necessarily the physical one).

This requires another mantra if it is to be achieved quickly.

The universe in its essential Divine essence then becomes more entwined in the seekers experience of human life.

Then awareness of Divinity, God or Higher Power, can become a stronger component of daily life experience.

The Heart mantras

Om will still remain as the supreme mantra, as it encompasses all - external, internal, and beyond.

Then one can add an *Ishta* Mantra - this is your chosen sound manifestation or representation of your Divinity. (Your *Ishta* or Lord).

For example, Hindu derived mantras are such as *Krishna, Rama,* or *Hari Om.* Other religions also have a range of mantras.

Divine in the body

A problem that seems to be common in spiritual seeking, is the issue of the bodily and mental needs, desires, and the gamut of the human condition.

Many aspects of religion, (and spiritual practice), have sought to somehow separate out the body/mind, disregard it, discipline it fiercely, or somehow transcend it all.

This seems to lead to endless struggle.

Therefore, the next step in the use of mantras is to seek incorporation of the body/mind into spiritual practices, and hence incorporation into the Divinity that is both within and external – no separation.

Certain mantras can be used for this step.

At this point it could be useful to do some reading on spiritual forces and healing forces within the body.

Knowledge about the chakras and kundalini is one place to start.

The purpose of spiritual practice, which unites the human forces or sublimates them, is to attain a harmonious loop of the human and the Divine - where human nature is not an obstacle, (or even "evil")

This practice where the merger of divine and human is sought is Tantric practice.

Tantric practice recognises the whole gamut of human emotion and nature, (but seeks to move to a higher level of being without denying human activity, such as sex).

Mantra over time

If one takes the time to study this topic in is some depth, one will find that there is a wealth of information and in-depth science of the power of a word. Each mantra from the ancient historical past of India has an author - a wise sage. It has a supernatural being that informs that transcendental component. It has an underlying seed form, or *bija*, which is the subtle unconscious power of that sound.

The sound itself is allied to a particular energy, (Shakti), which is the unseen vibration of that sound. This is somewhat similar to sound waves which can be heard when channelled through an instrument, (such as a radio). All of these components are held together by an unseen pillar or pin. (Just like the body held upright by the spine).

The mantra however must be awakened through its use by the person using it. So, a mantra could be merely supplementary to other spiritual practices, or vice versa. However, the mantra can be used as the key practice spiritually and also to achieve any other outcome that is sought. Sound produces forms through its vibrations, and the repetition of a particular mantra brings forth awareness of both the form that is meditated on and the purification that is sought. Logically any person using a mantra would want to use one that is representing a favoured deity, or materialistic outcome. The choice of form of one's

Deity or desired outcome, becomes one's choice of mantra.

The mantra can also be a refuge. Its repetition can allow release or escape from certain difficult mental problems or thoughts, and move the minds focus to a healthier location. Constant repetition or japa over a long period can enable a shift from a deep-seated negative personal perspective towards the higher planes of light and energy.

The mantra is of course a spiritual word, although you may hear that any word repeated has its own power. Logically, it does not make sense to repeat some obnoxious phrases. For instance, whilst eating dinner certain words could provoke unpleasant regurgitation! Logically it makes sense to repeat something sweet, light, and healthy -unless one has a death wish!

Types of mantras.

Om is well-known by many across the world. It is considered however by some teachers to be a mantra more suited for those of a monastic inclination. Other mantras are the names of ones preferred Deity. There is a plethora of mantras in Buddhism, untold numbers in Hinduism, and under a different schema many such uses of sacred words in other religions.

OM is considered to be the most important mantra, and longer mantras generally begin with OM.

It is a seed mantra. Other seed or bija Mantras can also be considered to be Goddess mantras, and they are part of the Tantric tradition. They are themselves a core element of Tantric practice.

It is considered by most teachers, that a mantra should be imparted by someone who has a teacher role, or specific knowledge and wisdom of this area. Certainly, mantras have been taken up from books, from inner intuition, by divine initiation (nonphysical teacher or deity), or by other means. That is usually beneficial, sometimes harmful, and generally not so helpful.

The Bija mantras including Om are considered to be more powerful and therefore more suitable to practitioners initiated into the wider lore of Yoga, Vedanta, and Tantra.

It is the repetition and practice that is most important, but this is still a part of whole mechanisms that are engaged in Japa. Therefore, alongside practice, and awareness and knowledge about use of mantras will help to ensure better outcomes.

It is deemed helpful to do Japa at a quiet time such as dusk or drawn, sitting in a quiet and comfortable place, using a good posture, and a distraction free environment. One can also use a rosary, or *Mala*, keep a log or count, use verbal or mental repetition, or even write.

Mantras to use

Om is a common root of all the other secondary Bija mantras. It is considered to be the highest of all mantras. As used in its pronounced state it is the outward form of what is really a subtle state of sound, not measurable by any scientific means. It is like the sound of space, the ether that pervades all that is beyond our senses and awareness. It is a place where there is no apparent movement, and yet there is a subtle vibration that signifies the transcendental Divinity. Om proceeds from deep down in the body at the level of the stomach and moves up towards the chakra between the eyebrows. It terminates with what is called the *Chandrabindu,* ("the point on the moon"). This is shown above the M letter like a quarter moon with a dot above it. As below.

The M sound moves into a subtle vibration and ends with that dot which is one with the Divine.

Om consists of A, U, and M. It signifies threes in a lot of areas. One such is the three states of consciousness: waking dream and sleep. Other bija mantras also end with the Chandrabindu. However their meanings are often somewhat obscured, simply because it is necessary to understand their connection with their *Devata,* (Deity), or form of the Divine. Knowledge of Shakti is needed, as well as practice in meditation on their meanings, which will reveal their spiritual connections and purification power.

Some of the bija mantras are:

ऐं Aim - the bija mantra of Saraswati, the goddess of learning.

ह्रीं Hrim - the bija mantra of Mahamaya, the goddess of power over the created universe (of illusion).

श्रीं Srim - the bija mantra of Lakshmi, the goddess of wealth (in its broadest sense).

क्रीं Krim - the bija mantra of Kali, the fierce goddess, who has power in a human sense.

क्लीं Klim - the bija mantra of Kameshwari, the goddess of desire or contentment and satisfaction.

These mantras should be used by one who has been initiated or who has knowledge of the Sanskrit language or has been initiated by other subtle higher energies or beings.

Some of the mantras which are considered more for "general use" are:

Hari Om

Rama, Rama

Hari Krishna

OM Namah Shivaya

Soham

So signifies God or Guru, and *ham* signifies oneself. Repetition is an acknowledgement of one's essential oneness with God and one's spiritual teacher. It is to be repeated as one takes a breath in for the first part, and as one exhales for the second. It is also to be repeated when one is already in a quiet calm space, which may require use of other spiritual exercises to achieve. With this mantra one can enter into an extremely deep transcendental calmness. The process of repetition with awareness of breath and deep meditation practice is the path of perfection – the *Siddha Yoga*.

Unlimited contentment is already within but may need significant endeavours to deal with the external demands in an effective way. That is where practice involving the kundalini and chakras may be useful.

ऐं ह्रीं श्रीं क्रीं क्रूं

Japa

Repletion is called japa, and this is what you want to be doing for Enlightenment Now.

Choose your mantra.

Do the japa.

Then more questions may arise following the practice of japa.

A mantra can be "tailor made" for the individual or may change as practice progress is.

Multiple mantras can be used as some mantras are prayers. They are "extended" mantras, and a longer prayer may proceed then repetition of a short mantra, (such as a "seed" mantra).

A Guru or Teacher at this point will be very useful!

Techniques

- Repeat the mantra anywhere, any time.
- Use quiet time when possible.
- Sit cross-legged at times if possible.
- Early morning is "prime time".
- Use a Mala or rosary when possible.

Remember

- All mantras have equal Power. (It is how you use them).
- Mantra is one with Higher Power, God, and Divinity.
- Japa of mantra will help wish attainment - even if regretted later!
- At the time of death mantra will be a lifeline, (pun intended!).
- Japa of mantra will give you Sanctuary.

- Will help shut the sense "doors" to enable meditation.
- Will help you Realize God in this life.

Meditate on the chakras

Use the seed mantras as below "attaching" them as the meditation goes *downwards* through the chakras.

As energy is released the kundalini then goes *upwards* to the crown of the head.

Crown	*Sahasraram* Chakra - OM
Brow (3rd eye)	*Ajna* Chakra - OM
Throat	*Vishuddha* Chakra - Aim
Heart	*Anahata* Chakra - Hrim
Solar plexus	*Manipura* Chakra - Shrim
Sacral	*Svadhisthana* Chakra - Krim
Root	*Muladhara* Chakra - Klim

Om (Source of all)

AIM – (pronounced Aiim), the Bija mantra of Saraswati, the goddess of learning. Has the power to enhance cognition and understand complex teachings.

HRIM - (pronounced Hreem), is the mantra of the Divine Maya. Through it we can control the illusion power of our own minds. Mahamaya, the goddess of power over the created universe (of illusion). Has the power to awaken and purify the heart and overcome obsession with illusory life content.

SHRIM - (pronounced Shreem), is a mantra of love, devotion and beauty, relating to Lakshmi, the Goddess of Beauty and divine grace, to give us the good things of life, including health. It aids in fertility and rejuvenation. Lakshmi is the goddess of wealth (in its broadest sense). Has the power to engender wealth in all its forms

KRIM - (pronounced Kreem), is the great mantra of Kali, has a special power relative to the lower chakras, which can both stimulate and transform. It a main mantra of the Tantra. It should be used with care. Kali, the fierce goddess, has power to destroy. Power and control over all sexual issues.

KLIM – (pronounce Kliim), the bija mantra of Kameshwari, the goddess of desire or contentment and satisfaction.

Thus the mantra is: OM AIM HRIM SHRIM KRIM KLIM (In that order)

These seed mantras are not rigidly applied but rather can be attuned to how you meditate. Thus, they could be used for personal wish or desire gratification. In Tantric views this is not necessarily "bad' – just practice at a base level. Ultimately in the Tantric view, such diversions are temporary, as the repetition of mantra will always want to lead to the high purified spiritual levels. At such levels one is moved more into the heart and higher chakras, and the Divine etheric space, above and around. Then the mantras of choice would change. OM or SOHAM are preferred. N.B. Some consider that Kundalini arises up and down fully and naturally in one continuous cycle.

ऐ ह्रीं श्रीं क्लीं हुं

Meditation and Mantras

This part is the summary about using mantras to enhance enlightenment.

We are already Divine.

Part of the Divine World.

However, we find ourselves in darkness.

Immersed in addictions, fear, depression, and anxiety.

We don't find or see our true nature until we can move past the darkness into the light. The darkness is still part of the universe and a very necessary part also.

So our journeys in darkness and out, have been necessary as part of our learning. We are now ready to be in our true space and place, and to experience this throughout our daily life and activities.

The mantra seeks to make our enlightenment a practical experience.

Something we can do through the body and mind down to the tips of our toes and through all emotional mental and physical states. The type of mantra that will work, requires that we understand the centres of our body.

In Sanskrit these are called chakras, which translate as "wheel". It's a centre that takes in and gives out energy. Chakras have been discussed in previous writings as well as a kundalini energy. (The energy that flows up and down between the centres.

Traditionally there are sounds associated with the chakras called bija mantras or seed mantras. However, the traditional seed sounds for the centres are not commonly used as "every day" mantras for chanting. (But certainly, as a meditation aid). Theoretically repeating those sounds help you achieve a deeper medication.

There is however another way to access the energy of the chakra so that the negative energy is moved up and out the body, and the divine energies move down to the specific chakra that is being focused upon.

This focus is achieved with another type of seed mantra. These mantras are allied to the Goddess Energy and to the spiritual path of Shakti, (Divine Energy seen as female in presentation). This is in essence a Tantric form of using mantras, as tantra means to "go out into the world".

The word *tantra* means to weave and simply is about applying the spiritual processes so as to be out in the world instead of seeking introspection. Yes, this does include sex! After all that is a major component of most human and other mammals' lives!

By using these seed mantras which relate to specific Divine energy or forms, which are also specific to a chakra, we can put our enlightenment to practice throughout the whole body.

As we meditate on all the chakras through the Shakti, (inherent energies), we release the negative power and receive the divine power. Tantric mantras can produce almost instantaneous results, due to the awakening of the kundalini, the primal energy or Shakti.

This spiritual growth however may seem negative in experience! When the chakras are awakened the negative energies within them come out.

The tendency is that addictions, fear, depression, and anxiety etc. can bubble to the surface and could thus create significant problems. (But eventually these are eliminated through the crown chakra at the top of the head).

This is a clearing process, but it can seem destructive temporarily. It can be also problematic if a person is practicing tantric kundalini awakening, using Bija mantras without guidance. That is why the teacher, guides or guru are important throughout the journey.

The topmost chakra, the crown chakra, (and also the Ajna chakra between the eyes), is allied to the "bench mark" mantra, AUM or OM, and is also a seed mantra. The prime mantra of them all! Unlike all the others OM is not specific to female/male energy.

If this is the sound of the universe, the Cosmic Soul, the Brahma, that transcends everything. It is the key mantra for renunciate monks, or sannyasins, as is enhances focus on the Divine in formless form, transcendent to the world and human life. Used on its own achieve awareness or knowledge of the formless God/Higher Power/Cosmic Consciousness.

These seed sounds have not been developed but arise naturally from the Cosmos and inhabit every part of our body, functioning to a specific rhythm, pulse, and purpose. Diagram explains both the "traditional: recognized sounds for chakras and the use of the tantric seed sounds for these chakras has been given above.

Goddess Inspired

Sahasraram Chakra
    Crown chakra (see note below).

Ajna Chakra   3rd eye - OM

Vishuddha Chakra
    Throat chakra – Energy of Sarasvati.

Anahata Chakra Heart Chakra. *Maya* energy.

Manipura Chakra
    Solar plexus chakra. Lakshmi is the Goddess.

Svadhisthana Chakra   Sex chakra. Kali. Goddess

Muladhara Chakra
    Root (or Earth) chakra

The Maya energy is in the heart chakra. Maya or *Mahamaya* as the Goddess, is the loci of our illusion, the world and the created universe. Seems real! Then seems to change, then vanish. Our dreams disappear. Our lives disappear! It's real enough to the unenlightened person, but really, we are not solid bodies at all! (Check Quantum physics for the scientific perspective regarding the atom "dance" of so-called solid matter).

Next chakra is associated with the Goddess of wealth, or position, or even food, in the navel area, extending around the stomach area. Without food there is no life, and no offspring, (the fundamental "possession"). Lakshmi is the Goddess energy associated here. This energy includes also sexual and blissful elements. Then the two lower chakras are associated with the sexual energies as well as the "dark" Goddess Kali

The repetition, of Bija mantra, is thus to be allied specific to each chakra, but this is not frequently expanded in ancient traditions and is quite a secret teaching! Treatises about this topic are usually hard to find!

Om or AUM has always been associated with the third eye or the spot between the eyebrows even when it has not been associated with kundalini energy or chakras. It is also seen by some as connected to the crown chakra, especially when the sound "trails off " in the long "M" AH is also for the crown chakra, but practitioners of the OM chanting may wish to focus on the final drawn out "M" sound of OM, trailing off into the crown and then out to the ether. This is a very powerful meditation, which may not come easily until other centres have been purified using other sounds.

OM is thus the most well know and expansive of the bija mantras as it leads into the "soundless" *Akasha* space, which is the "etheric" quality of the universe. This leads to formless *Samadhi* (deepest meditation without thought forms). It can cause the Shakti energy to surge upward and outward beyond the Kundalini chakras.

As used in its pronounced state it is the outward form of what is really a subtle state of sound, not measurable by any scientific means. It is like the sound of space, the ether that pervades all that is beyond our senses and awareness. It is a place where there is no apparent movement and yet there is a subtle vibration that signifies the transcendental Divinity.

The seed mantras are part of tantric lore, Goddess worship, Shakti/ kundalini contain a power in a broad sense. Thus, the seed mantras should also be considered in terms of both external focussed meditation and for the "reverse" flow of energy back down the body through the chakras. This is an essential concept of Tantra and helps spirituality to be" seeped' intimately to all parts of the body-based life journey.

Kundalini and Shakti

Kundalini is otherwise known as the serpent power, which is considered to be like a coiled snake of energy at the base of the spine. It can be coiled there in a dormant state and when awakened the energy or Shakti arises in a sinuous movement through the centre of the spine to the crown of the head. Along the way are centres of energy called chakras and each one of those chakras has specific and particular attributes.

Shakti is also considered to be the universal energy or Goddess energy - the creation force of the divine being. In this sense the masculine aspect of divine being is seen as a transcendental power which is beyond form and shape and the female aspect is seen as the external creation. When practitioners worship the Shakti or Goddess form, they can worship the divine being as the world, the universe, or creation.

Some schools of thought and philosophy accept only one monotheistic divinity. Those with an interest in kundalini and Shakti view the female aspects as either continuous with the male transcendent or as coexisting. Religious belief is of course included in this dimension. In Hinduism in the Vedanta philosophy, there is only one unified Divine being and creation is sometimes called Maya or other words representing an illusory universe. This is in the sense of illusion as being something to be transcended, or even avoided, in order to realise the Divine knowledge and truth, (as per Vedanta philosophy). In this case only the transcendental locus has truth. Vedanta means the end of the Vedas and was developed as a swing away from ritualistic practice in ancient Indian times.

For those who are devotees of the Goddess then, manifested Shakti is the way of liberation or achievement of higher consciousness. It involves partaking of all that the world offers even though the final goal is liberation and freedom from birth and death (or rebirth). Such practitioners are called *Shaktas* - the worshippers of Shakti or the Goddess. The path is also the Tantric path because the Tantric path is simply spirituality with full acceptance of the world and one's place in it as a human being. As a human being the whole gamut of desires, needs, and goal focused activities etc., is seen as needing to be both understood as well as transcended. Kundalini is involved in both the Tantric focus as well as the practices of a Siddha, because a Siddha will have ability, control, and knowledge regarding the kundalini, the nature of desire and involvement in the world, and the way through (using the world), to a higher spirituality.

Some consider that the kundalini rises up from the sleeping coiled state only when awakened through yogic practices, or by the special grace of a teacher who obviously has the Siddha powers, (*Siddhis*), to make this happen. Some practitioners say that a highly developed spiritual person has naturally free-flowing energies, and the kundalini rises up through all the chakras and freely moves past the crown chakra into the sacred ether to a transcendental state. Then the energy of the divine being or the higher power revolves back down into the body, purifying all the centres. Some yogis will however practice activities to make controlled and channelled energy rise up through the chakras, using meditation on the chakras centre, whilst using mantras to purify each location. Kundalini can therefore be moved as a continuous flow upwards as well as downwards, free flowing without blockage.

Whatever practice chosen, the reality for most is that the road of spiritual practice can be a lengthy one, with a lot of repetition, endeavour and discipline. It may be possible to get to one's goal of connection with God in one hit as in becoming "born-again" and then move on from this life into a permanent spiritual space, such as that called Heaven. For others it may take many revolving lifetimes of practice to truly achieve liberation from the cycle of birth and death. Either way simply believing one is in enlightened, or in touch completely with one's highest God or Divinity, may not be an actual reality. Some of those professing such perfection seem to have not been able to overcome or manage some basic common human frailties. The way of the Tantric practitioner or the worshipper of the goddess energy, is to accept the human nature and work with it, not against it, until it there is true proof of purification, and the practitioner sits in a natural spiritual state of bliss and knowledge

There are libraries almost of literature about kundalini and Shakti, and there are many teachers in this field. Any search including using Internet, will generate enough information to keep an interested person busy for years.

What does not come so easily is the inside knowledge about the workings of kundalini and Shakti, or the use of sacred sounds including bija mantras. A Siddha will know the secret: the inside knowledge of the area and will know how certain sounds go with certain chakras, or work in certain ways to develop one's ability to both function in the world and to transcend it. Getting the free flow of kundalini may be considered by some to be relatively easy, but this does not of itself guarantee that a practitioner is freed from many years of struggle. It is here and now in the body, in the daily grind of life business that the work still occurs. Not just to survive or then flourish in human terms, but also to have a human ability to be a spiritual soul rather than just a physically embodied one.

When the practitioner freely moves up and down through the chakras with true purification, it becomes easier to focus and be on the higher levels. At that point the locus of meditation can become the heart, and the higher centres become a route through which divine energy revolves, descends and moves out to others. At this point other and mantras and meditations may be preferred by the practitioner.

The use of specific bija mantras may speed up true purification and achievement of the higher levels.

Siddha Swami

What is a Siddha Swami?
You may have heard of the word or name – Swami.
A swami is a renunciate, a person who has renounced the world and become a monk.
Literally it means someone who has transcended the ego – *swa* (give up or surrender), *me* (myself). So, *Swami is* really about a person's attributes and not what cloth they wear.
A swami (traditionally in Hinduism), wears ochre red or similar colour robes, signifying a body and mind that is being "burnt up" by the fire of renunciation. The word Siddha means a perfected being or one with powers. Therefore, the Siddha Swami is one who is the spiritually enlightened being with some power or abilities, (preferably to enable the transformation of others), and not one who has merely attained some yogic state or power.

A true guru is a Sat (true or only one), Guru (teacher). A Perfected Teacher, who is a Divine being as one who has reached the state of oneness with the Divinity, (sometimes known as God).

Some see this sort of human incarnation as being in the form of Jesus, as God becomes human, or in the form of Buddha, a human being made perfect by his own endeavour, as one who has entered the state of Nirvana. Nirvana or Moksha is a state of both enlightenment and freedom, (from birth and death). Some see such a one as their own teacher, of whatever spiritual path or religion they have chosen.

In India there are many holy persons who practice austerity and penance, meditate and follow a variety of spiritual paths, while garbed as a swami. There are quite a few who are seen as Siddhas by their devotees, and a number who have a large international following. Some of these beings attain that goal they seek and become perfected, in the eyes of their followers, without necessarily presenting in a monastic role or environment. They are considered perfected in the eyes of their adherents, whatever religion, country, and role they manifest in and are present in.

All such beings can teach humanity to not just be "ordinary", but also to strive to attain the same place where they sit. A place of Divine state of awareness.

Siddhas teach that any of us can and should attain a state of spiritual perfection whilst remaining in the human condition.

The caveat is that the Siddha is more than and dominates any swami role. Therefore, the soul that has that Siddha power and ability, and is in the enlightened domain, does not need to follow the typical practice or external presentation of a monastic practitioner.

One who has achieved that state quite naturally is in renunciation mode and is not swayed by the external world- particularly by desire, greed and lust.
Therefore, that soul does not need to wear red, as the fire burns fiercely inside.
He or she can be in any predicament or situation or country or lifestyle or role in the external world.

The Siddha being transcends the external world, which is seen as Maya. The Sanskrit word Maya means illusory, transient or temporary, in terms of the world which as a place of delusion and dream.

ut the Siddha is like a swan on the water floating and staying dry. In Sanskrit this is known as a *Paramahamsa* (Great Swan). That is to say the one who's in the world but not in the world - just floating on and above it. Still a human being, but with a certain supreme spiritual attainment. This does not deny the reality that the person who achieves may have been previously a so-called "ordinary" human being and is also one who still has the potential to present as an ordinary human being.

It is considered in Hinduism that the human birth is the place where one has potential to achieve what is called Nirvana or Moksha, and thus the final birth - with freedom from the bondage of endless cycles of birth and death.
This human life thus has spiritual meaning when used for all endeavours to transcend the human condition, even though humanistic service orientated endeavours are also seen as uplifting and beneficial.

Other religions even if not acknowledging or agreeing with this philosophy and perspective still exhort us to use our lifespan for spiritual and religious purpose.

A born-again person is deemed to rebirth into a spiritual world, whilst still experiencing and journeying through the physical and mental spheres. There are of course certain activities and practices that have to be followed if one is to attain the highest goal whilst travelling in the world. Spiritual endeavour and practice is required. There are of course certain conditions and circumstances that are required to achieve progress on the spiritual path

I describe the experience and areas of practice that ensued in my ten years as a monk in India. I have found both necessary and beneficial to base my practice in the way of the Siddha Swami on information gleaned in those years, and on a further 40 plus years study and development.

This way described is based on Siddha Yoga, Tantric pathways, Kundalini yoga, western and eastern religious and spiritual practices, the worship of a personal deity or God, and the realities of life experience in the human world.
It is also personal summary provided to assist any person on the spiritual path where possible.

There is no content which is entirely new - it's being more of a "personal recipe"! There are also many texts books and sources of information available to anyone who wishes to study in depth the topics touched on. Therefore, I am essentially describing my own spiritual adventure and progress, in terms of what I have experienced studied and learnt. Everyone's journey will be different, and I make no claim to having the "right path".

This writing also connects to my book, *English-Man, Holy-Man, Beggar-Man,* as well as document some of my experience as a monk. There is a planned continuation of these themes, of seeking and practising the path towards one's own spiritual goals.

The Components of the Siddha Path.

One

A guru - the true guru or Sat Guru

A human connection is usually needed to facilitate easily access the Divine (as the inner soul or the external deity), and the true guru manifests energy by grace). This enables the journey to proceed. For some this guru is the teacher who has moved on from human life (i.e. dead)! What remains is a significant force, as in one such as Jesus or the Buddha.

For others this being is someone who is still here and whom they still follow and receive instruction from. For others an amalgamation of a number of teachers is experienced. For others guidance comes from within - an inner teacher or a force that seems to be external.

The Siddha embodies a human based form of Divinity, but some will talk to God or other "angelic" or similar manifestation through an Inner Voice mechanism, that does the work of Guru and guidance for that individual.

The guru is "one who dispels darkness" (by adding Gu to Ru, where Gu means darkness), which is the centre core function of a Siddha

Maybe not totally, or maybe in some areas, (in the case of a "partial" Siddha with power and ability to a limited extent), the energy sought will be that which is needed for the guidance of the individual at a particular time.

Therefore there may be several teachers who each guide in way their own specific and special way.

There is always a lineage of some sort except in the case of exceptional teachers who seem to materialise out of nowhere for the sake of the century or multiple centuries.

Either way or whatever the scenario, turning a human to the Divine makes the guide process work so much more spontaneously and effectively. If the one who seeks has an understanding of the guru function and purpose. The Divine or Divine perfection or even some minor Siddhis powers, or even material gain (if one seeks this), are more accessible with the receipt of the guru grace. This grace dispels "darkness", negativity, "stuckness", and even gloom and despair.

Even if you want to learn a trade or get a degree or make some money, there is always a need for a guide/teacher.

Two

In the path of the Siddha there is a need to understand the spirit force that flows through the body

In the traditional meditation on kundalini, this energy is seen as coiled at the base of the spine like a serpent, and it arises to pass through certain centres or chakras throughout the body.

This energy is also known as a form of Shakti (power or energy), and is an energy manifested in the human form, which has significant connection and contexts with the Goddess powers within the Hindu domain, and within some forms of Buddhism.

The awakening of the kundalini is also connected directly with the Sat Guru, because it is the guru who can bestow *Shakti-Paat*. This is a kind of a "beaming out of power", which awakens another person's kundalini. This is a key Siddhi of the Siddha guru. With this "power shower" to awaken the source, one can awaken kundalini directly, to rise up through the chakras, and travel beyond the final chakra in the crown of the head.

Otherwise personal experience of this energy may be problematic, because there may be traumatic issues involved in the passage of this energy through the chakras, where this is awoken without direction, guidance and oversight. (Would a student doctor perform complex surgery?)

However, whatever scenario is involved, once practice takes place, the attainment of Divine realisation through Kundalini Yoga requires full attenuation of awareness, and astute management of the process, to experience the kundalini energy in only positive and beneficial ways.

Three

In Sanskrit, spiritual practice is called *Sadhana*. This is necessary to enable the practice of going within to flourish. It is also necessary to practice when seeking the Divine force as manifested externally.

There are many views of what God, is or how the Higher Power, the Divine spiritual being, can be attained.

Religions are many, and there are many single or multiple options are available for the spiritual practitioner to choose from. One needs to not just to choose some way, but to get actively moving along ones chosen path.

Some say you must follow only one path only or one way. In reality many people follow different paths at different times in their lives. It does seem logical to keep on one focused way, but then human life is not always logical.

People also change their religion.

However, what is advisable is to have guide, so that whatever paths/s are taken, they can be followed with some certainty, just as if one has one has a map to read.

It is somewhat similar to treating disease. The correct medication has to be found, and sometimes it is necessary to change or adjust medication and the dosage. Therefore, it is not uncommon to have more than one spiritual teacher. Or to change or move on from a particular teaching.

So, what is best-is what works for you, as long as you do the practice.

Within spiritual practice there is also need to adopt specific methods that work for each unique individual. One travels paths, but one also uses different means to attain movement. Such as car, a horse, or a camel. What form of meditation or specific type of yoga will you personally adopt? One could ask a similar question in Christianity -will it be Methodist or Catholic or some other?

The traditional path of the *Siddha Marg, the* perfected being pathway, in Hinduism, has been to use the power of the kundalini and of mantras (sacred word or sounds). In this Dark Age, (*Kali Yuga*), the repetition of the chosen mantra is deemed to be the easiest way to obtain spiritual power and focus for self-realisation.

Japa is repetition of a mantra whereas *dhyana* is meditation on what that mantra means. It is a distilled form of a complex chant or prayer and a simple form that can be repeated at any time silently mentally, verbally, or on even on a subtler level.

Four

A force not often mentioned, is that is that of life experience, as a force that has "power over us".

Without life in our experience we do not exist, we do not get to achieve some of our desires, nor do we partake of spiritual paths. Also, human lives seem to present us with lessons and a means to move from gross experience of the body mind to subtler levels.

There is a powerful spiritual force behind our life, if we accept the challenge of our problems. That means including mental disorders, addictions, relationship and psychological problems. In other words, the whole gamut of what can seem "just insane". If we deal with life as it is and allow teachers in, we can also move through and find a purposeful momentum or motivation to walk the spiritual path.

Everything can have purpose for our spiritual destiny, even whatever seems bad or desperate. What is seemingly devoid of any credit may also have its purpose, or may produce a lesson. To learn about what is painful is a start. Not all knowledge necessarily comes from good things, nor understanding from doing what is right.

The whole area of life passages is the subject of multiple books and other media that is available in the field of "self-help" or "personal growth". The personal journey is a very popular subject and there are many bestsellers in this field. People want to deal with their lives and become happy or at least not be unhappy, sooner or later.

I have written about my own experience of life as it has connected me further to deeper into my spiritual search and practice

In summary the Siddha is a beacon for the path to both God and to perfected development of the human purpose. The Siddha is a representative of the divine, and the Siddha path is a way set for us by the lineages and the numbers of Siddhas who have made themselves servants to our spiritual development.

Gurus have their differing level of ability, but all present us with something that meets our need at particular times. They can present as a fairly ordinary persons also, but there will be a profound depth of spiritual practice and knowledge radiating from some inner enlightenment. That will shine and be a core more powerful than any external practice or monasticism. This is about life here, but also about transcending it.

Off - floating above the sea of life- the Paramhansa.

Parama means great and *Hansa* means swam. The "Great Swan", can float on the water without getting wet, and the Paramahansa guru thus is in the world but "untouched" by it. Or this "swan" can separate milk from water or separate the cream from the whey - as per mythology!

Kundalini, depression and medicine

Kundalini works in the body through the chakra centres. It flows and allows blocks to move. That is physical, psychological, mental, and emotional. Everything.

This can pay out, in the broadest sense. Hopefully, to increase Bliss.

Suffering and Bliss. How these words resonate within the religious or spiritual sphere. Kundalini revealed and free to flow is synonymous with a deep spiritual awareness, and a connection with the Divine. However, at some point the full process of energy involvement through the centres or chakras becomes irrelevant. We may do our daily spiritual practice, move into the sphere of knowledge and awareness of a Oneness around us. So really the whole idea of human awakening "upwards" through the chakras can be dispense with, or reversed, as one becomes more proficient. The same Divine energy comes down to enable a somewhat different, but still Divine experience. From a religious perspective we worship the Divine firstly as external deity, and as a powerful being. We are at risk of being the ostrich. With head buried in the sand, if we are not aligned to Divine energy presenting into our human lives, mentally and physically, *as our own essential being or nature*. So, the idea of meditating on kundalini arising only may be somewhat misleading.

The external teacher or guru can help with clarification. Will this be Jesus, the Buddha, or our own Gurus or any source that we seek for guidance? Remember that we are already connected to the Divine, because we are already part of a Divine universe. This can be seen in the sense that a spark is not different in essence to the fire.

Many who write about kundalini talk of periods of despair and feelings of failure. It seems similar to reports of religious experience that at senior stage of practice, God seems to turn away. Such descriptions have a very strong correlation to that of depression as a psychiatric disorder, characterized by specific symptomatology. The connection of spirituality and depression, or a deep abyss, seems there, but what about this in terms of kundalini energy. What about our own levels of enlightenment, for does a rising and hence weakening of kundalini, and the descending of Divine energy, really awaken deep consciousness in the body. This is in some conflict with many taught aspects of kundalini practice. However, the purpose and function of kundalini awakening should be ultimately, to enable us to have an experience of the *witness stage*, where we "see through" life, and see it *as it is*. Ultimately, because this is the *Gyana* stage or self-knowledge stage.

The kundalini is a holy force aligned to the Goddess energy. Otherwise, might be similar to the Holy Spirit. It takes us out of our material craziness, but also it takes us through them, not passing by them or burying them. The Awakening doesn't make us mad or bad, we already were.

We do however, have to take what cure we really need to take, and leave what we can discard. For instance, much of religion has become distorted over the years, and often serves no purpose or, confuses and even destroys us. We need then to see religion as something that can help us only in parts.

Does Prozac have a place? Does Valium have a place? Or, do we get a therapist? Herbalist, crystal gazer, acupuncturist, psychiatrist, hypnotist? The options are multiple, but the opinions are even more so. Some believe psychiatry is the work of the Devil. For some it's New Age that is the devil. In short, degrees of fundamentalism are very common. It is actually all around us in many forms and even is the new norm!

Kundalini yoga is supposed to be therapeutic. There is some research into its practice, of course quite a lot of research looks at the value of meditation. Writers in this field have expressed views that the kundalini process can include physical and mental problems. They also agree that the kundalini process can lead to the unveiling of the true self and enlightenment.

Depression may be located in the heart chakra, but its effects appear to be in the brain area. The right side of the heart is described as a true spiritual centre. A number of teachers are very clear on this view. Depression also has echoes in monasticism and renunciation. The Sanskrit word *vairagya* means dispassion. In this case it is almost a complete abhorrence of the world that drives a person into the state of renunciation known as *sannyas*. This is very similar to the state of anhedonia, which is in psychiatry is a loss of interest in all the world that previously appeared attracting. The early life of the Buddha also illustrates this overwhelming urge through, "sadness", to remove oneself from the world at all costs, even if one was a king. One view could be that he had a very low mood, the second of the two main symptoms of clinical depression.

The connection between the centre of the heart, and the right side of the body, is an esoteric subject all of its own. The product of these two areas may reflect a conflict between this life of the family, society and the male/female domain, and the domain of monasticism, and introspection. Its cave vs the cafe! Or, we could see also a focus on good vs evil.

This primary chakra, however, may be more than just one chakra. It seems to be an area that is also reached after the crown chakra has been breached. A sort of umbrella of light then moves down from the head to the heart area, and then all around the body. Then the right–side heart chakra in the sense of the kundalini structure could be seen as different, and as a centre attained *after the kundalini has risen up, out and then flowed back down –externally.* It is difficult to explain, as it seems that the experience comes about as a result of advance meditation practices.

Can the concept of depression, connected to kundalini and spiritual awakening, be seen as a higher process that is trying to connect and balance both of flow and of energy to and from divine consciousness? This view meets the needs and aspirations of the human personality that whilst spiritually seeking, also suffers issues with mood, anxiety, fear and reactivity.

In present society moving into an era of ever exponentially advancing research, approaches to medical treatment to mental health may come to a recognition of kundalini type "electricity". If currently medication approaches stay limited in their effectiveness, it needs be that the true workings of the brain are found, and the consequent cures thus "discovered".

Then kundalini energies may be recognized, just as the power of meditation and other spiritual practice is being "discovered". At this point we can say that psychiatric drugs to some degree are toxins that may damage the brain, whilst healing the disorders. This is no different than saying that paracetamol or aspirin is harmful. Just because we may say that psychiatry is defunct, we can also say the same about religion, or new age, or spiritual practice. In reality if we have medication that helps us to some degree, and personally we can benefit without significant side effects, there should be no conflict between our spiritual practice and scientific evidence-based medicine. (Particularly, but not exclusively, speaking here for the use of anti-depressants).

Chapter 3
Goddess Inspired..............................

The Essence

The essence of being is here and now. It is connected with some sense of Divinity. What you either believe or experience is different. Ones experience of Divinity is possibly very similar to anyone else's, as its only one and the same Divinity. Whereas a great a difference in belief variation occurs. Each individual is different here from anyone else, but it does not seem to be much value in having a religion that is separate from another religion for instance. Go and look at DNA and see where we all started from, and yes I wonder why then we need war. Separation of any sort is to be avoided for the purposes of being enlightened. It's probably non-productive also, and that is another good, Divine reason.

Without a Cosmic Consciousness, it is pointless even think about global harmony, although serenity and peace are attainable in varying degrees. It's still a here thing, and nothing else is just a mess, or leaning towards chaos. How does one attain this state? Actually, it's probably more about how one is avoiding it. It's probably about being a so normal human, so just stop doing that crazy stuff and move towards the divine within oneself!

Well maybe one cannot stop doing the crazy stuff. Remember the idea about being powerless over addictions, as espoused in A.A. and N.A.? This reality of just being powerlessness filters down probably into all aspects of our lives but inflamed by ego we don't recognise or accept much of this. If things get bad enough then you can accept a solution, any solution, if it gets bad enough. The solution may be seen as surrender to God, or to some higher power - possibly. Or, we see a way out through therapy, psychiatry, and even throw in a little medication!

It is also possible to throw enlightenment away, as we are probably experiencing a lot of divine moments without even noticing the spirit is here. It's actually all around us, through us, inside, outside. Wherever.

There is a choice to allow our guides to say what is okay, and what is not. A guide is just you, (or rather an "inside" voice), but you see it as slightly or very separate. The guide as you, as a Divine Being can be experienced, when all life is Divine. And any individual part is beyond human description, (such as being awesome). So, accept the guru or guide, as you accept your inner thoughts. If you don't have an external guide or have moved on from that, you will "hear" the inner guiding voices as you persist on your chosen spiritual path.

You're saying, stop those thoughts. Why? Because those thoughts are not needed. I'm home now. They go around the brain, where they have no function except to generate reactivity, and anxiety. Why are they there? Good question. I'm just in a play, and they just are part of the dream, and you know it inside, in your Truth. Your thought processes connected to body messages leverage your human experience. You may want to just leave them alone and try and get through the day, and most people do just this. The human experience - that is just what you accept as a given. After all that is why we are here? You may say "maybe" to this?

Perhaps it's just desire to be a human form, and to stay that way, no matter how painful. Or, it's just an inheritance decreed by cosmic forces, or a God. (Or, "its karma man"). It's all very mysterious at times, though the followers of any particular religion always want to give you a specific answer that "solve" everything. That is their choice of direction in life. Which may also help to drive you more bonkers!

The Buddha says life is suffering.

If you get that and feel it badly, you probably can be diagnosed as clinically depressed. Take some medication, or if it gets really bad, don't get the electrical shock treatment. There are more "modern" options coming out, including micro-dosing of psychedelics. Best not to get the label of a mental disorder and keep out of that system if possible.

You will be fine. Back to work, and society and all that. Otherwise, you may end up on the street, or as an alcoholic. See how you can be judges or self-judge!

However, the Guides say you are Divine. I am Divine. Who is Divine? All is Divine

Do you want to accept this, and what would that mean?

It doesn't mean anything other than me and you as we always were. Just Enlightened!

A simple, I Am.

Therefore, one needs a guide, a good teacher. Unless you are already there.

Although, yes, the guru is still human with potentially more foibles than you have.

It is the teaching or guidance that is wanted. Grab that and ignore and rest!

Here is the mantra to get the inner and outer guru advice and guidance. Repeat it and the guru will come to you in peace with offerings.

OM GURU OM

Sanctuary

I have sought the Sanctuary. It has become a driving need, as I am propelled by a reaction to the physical human world. Fear, anxiety, depression, have all played a part in pushing me to seek Sanctuary. I feel as if I am being driven, herded, and see a Divine force is the instigator.

The force of the Divine, (my preferred word), is the real driver, although to all intents and purposes I tended to believe that I am master and controller of my life. I am in charge. I have choices. However, I can also admit that I have zero power, that I am desperate and empty of all abilities to control or manage anything, one iota.

I have found the Sanctuary. It is a gift of the Divine, a place to feel safe - a haven. I was initially angry that I could not be there physically, and that I had still be here in this world full of "nonsense". However, I found that I was still procrastinating, trying to bargain, and being heedless and ungrateful of the help I was receiving from the Divine. But I still sought to take my physical being also into the Sanctuary. I started to feel this as so even whilst embodied. How can this be so? How can I be in heavenly spirit-based space and also be on the planet? Hard to explain on paper or in writing.

This is a meditation process. Meditation is not wholly disconnected from life and vice versa. For some the whole spiritual process is life,-and the no-spirituality is death. For some meditation is just an exercise for good health - like going to the gym. To make a choice here just ask - are we spirit, or are we flesh?

Sanctuary is a cure, a very big cure! It is a personal cathedral and temple. It is where safety is guaranteed, and where the body can also go whilst in a contemplative or meditative position. The advance practice is to bring Sanctuary into real waking and walking life. To be in Sanctuary, whilst not being particularly contemplative or meditative. (Like to have one's cake and eat it). It is to be freed from endless wandering in the wilderness-sometimes known as the daily drudge. It is also practical in the sense of having problem with daily needs.

How can, what is just an exercise in meditation or spiritual visualisation, engender such an overarching, all-encompassing relief. There is no doubt that it needs to be so. It needs to be a sanctuary for the needy, not just a place or space when all is well and the sun is shining. It is not being on a lovely beach, cocktail in hand with waiters hovering, and a gold-plated credit card on the platter. It has to be do-able at the bottom of the pit when the very meaning or purpose of life is very fragile, if not broken.

Sanctuary needs to be a better pain fix than any drug, drink, or pleasuring activity. Otherwise, it is not a true sanctuary. It needs to be a cure for what ails one.

How does one get to this wonderful healing place? You could seek answers to this question through some religious pathway. Just talk to your local fundamentalists!

"No problem- Jesus Saves."

"My guru has the answers."

"Follow the Buddha"

They may be right to a degree, but they don't offer sanctuary directly without the middlemen. (Usually men!). The fundamentalists make a fundamental mistake that God's property belongs to a specific religion, belief, or practice. Sanctuary is the property of the Divine. It belongs to no one, and is available to anyone. It can be requested, sought, desired, or contemplated on in prayer meditation, or just in distress. It is available to any believer in the Divine represented as God, Higher power, *Brahman* etc., and quite likely available to any who seek help without specific beliefs.

I found it through and after many years of religious and spiritual endeavour, culminating in a state of total desperation, with a strong wish to be out of this world. One could say that my fifty years of searching practise had bought me little success. However, there is more here than it seems, and more toto be added about the value of spiritual striving and searching. Sanctuary is coming home, into the abode of one's own Divine presence. It is also about being held there. It does not and should not be a heaven that you can only get to after death. It is here and now if you want it.

The meaning of life

The human is a speck in a living Universe.

That Universe has a personal connection and availability to any human.

It is not a matter of faith but of trust. The Divine is all around, with and without and cannot be "overrun" by human science, ideas, or endeavours.

The purpose of life is to be in a trusting embrace within the Divine. This is the only meaning of life.

The means to achieve this symbiosis is freely available. Choose your pathway. There are many. Spiritual endeavour is what is needed per individual. It also means and requires that spiritual endeavour is not distracted by claims, fundamentalist views, or religious and spiritual superiority complexes. Practice does make perfect.

The Divine has been here on Earth in human form. It is now time for the human form is to become Divine. Science and progress will never alter the essential human dilemma. Death is a foregone conclusion for all. We can delay it and improve on the lot of the human life condition. Many however remain living in abject misery all around us-even as we improve the lot of some, which always seems to be the entitled minority. It is not the fault of scientists, humanistic psychology and endeavour, or progress, (in its broadest sense). All are well meaning and seek to improve the experience and quality of life. However, the self-centred human nature will remain predominant in the world and continue to lead to a minority getting the most of the pie, as and when any opportunity presents. The solution remains then for individuals to enter into the Divine. This removes human motivation from human negativity and self-seeking, and will benefit the planet on subtle levels, beyond the works of all well-meaning humanistic endeavours. This will be the energy that engenders a green society!

Spiritual endeavours include prayer, meditation, chanting, worshipping, and a wide range of activity that takes the soul from the mind body construct towards a Presence, which is beyond all comprehension. Quantity of spiritual endeavour is important. A practice is needed that can be joined with multiple occasions per day. Personal prayers or chants that you can do at any time. Traditional religion does have already some good options here, but in this post modernistic world we have a supermarket of potential pathways at our fingertips. A holy place one can visit or attain will reflect the Divine Sanctuary. Healing options may be of the evidence-based scientific systems, or otherwise. The history of modern evidence-based scientific focused medicine was really started in ancient monasteries and ashrams. In those days, evidence and science were what the sages proposed in their own Enlightened way.

Religion and the Spiritual Journey

Theoretically the spiritual journey could be made without any references to or
 involvement with religion, either as belief or practise or as morals. I have not seen, met, or read of any spiritual advanced being, who was not at some stage intimately involved with religion in some form.

Religion and spiritual practice seem to go hand in hand, although on a closer inspection this relationship is quite tenuous and even hostile. The spiritual seeker may find at a certain stage a burning desire or motivation to escape from or leave behind all or some of previously held beliefs and practices. In some religions this is ok, in others it is high treason. The Zen Buddhist for instance have a saying "if you meet the Buddha on the road, kill him"! They seem to be implying that at the higher stage of spiritual practise, you move on from even the teachers and teachings that you started out with.

In Hinduism too there is a tradition of the naked yogis who though revered as very holy, give up all moral, and social/religious restraints ad practises. This "madness" of the crazy adepts in spiritual tradition, is practised by people who have been immersed in some form of religious culture, and then metaphorically or literally cast off their clothes. In some religious cults, any deviance from the accepted moral and social rules is seen as a fall from grace, a sin, and gross deviation. Spirituality there is only accepted in the context of the rules. However, it is a fact that no one religion has the control over the world population that its more fanatic adherents would wish for. Some spiritual seekers have and always will hold onto their own faith. Even if allegiance to a religion is shattered or becomes insignificant.

The Spiritual Journey is about the goal, the end product, notwithstanding the connections made on the way with organised religion, New Age ideas, and scientific therapies. Religion becomes a block to spiritual growth when it interferes with, or is allowed to block, further evolvement. The concept of God, Deities, Messiahs and Avatars, (incarnations), belongs to the realm of the practitioner, not to the world of the Realiser, who has become Awakened, Enlightened or Divinely fulfilled. That goal is really quite anarchic, disinhibited, and even destructive in terms of what passes as conventional ways of equating an ordinary life with the Higher Power. Most materialistic everyday strivings seem to be geared to trying to get on with or outwit God in order to achieve ends. God then becomes someone or something "up there", and the church or temple becomes a convenient place to off load the guilt or shame generated, whilst trying to fulfil basically selfish needs and wishes.

Spirituality does not require a God "up there", nor an edifice to worship in to prove one's goodness to others. The spiritual seeker then, is concerned with how to achieve the goal of Truth. How to begin the journey, (avoiding the obstacles and dead ends). How to find a good path and how to keep on it, whilst avoiding the distractions consolations that divert one. In that light all responsibilities are scrutinised, including the value of the religious devotional paths. This examining then becomes a form of yoga, a meditation, and philosophical enquiry.

Devotion which derives from or is associated with the East (Hindu, Buddhism and others), can be contrasted with the Western civilisation, or the modernity of scientific based beliefs, as well as the tradition of Christian and Jewish monotheism. More recent advent of the "psychological" forms of treatment and the therapies, which have evolved with the fields of mental health, also now propose themselves as holding solutions to life itself in a broader outreach. Many of the new age practises, and therapy modes, seem to be amalgamating and synthesising a total radical approach to the concept of wellbeing and "awareness". (Is this being "Woke"?). This would seem to be the good reason for their wide appeal to different body of spiritual practitioners, due to presenting this rather new outlook on what is "spiritual wellness".

Enlightenment Occurring

Enlightenment occurs when it is simply accepted!

That's it! No searching. No seeking. No spiritual trip. No materialistic trip.

The searcher is just that. The need for spiritual or material solace and comfort, is just that. Enlightenment occurs when all that stops. When all diversion, digression, and blocking stops. The nature of being is Enlightenment. It is our natural state. Our inherent always present, always active state. All the spirituality, religions, yogic, psychiatric, and personal growth trips are but efforts to remove, clear away, or breakthrough the stuff that coves our natural state.

Of themselves the practices have no meaning, although that is where most people are enmeshed in their own beliefs and practices, which are taken as the "end "rather than the means. This applies to all paths, gurus, teachers, gods and prophets. Anything, even the purest, most elevated holy forms of existence, cover over the native natural state of all beings, which is Enlightenment, as Truth, Knowledge, Bliss. Sat. Chit, Ananda.

This native state known, discussed, was written about for thousands of years from the time of the Vedas in ancient India (prior to Christ and Buddha). It has been called in Sanskrit, Sat, Chit, Ananda. (Truth/Knowledge/Bliss). This native state has, often as an "undercurrent", been expounded upon eloquently at great length by all the major world religions (although often in "hidden or secret tracts"). For all those few that have sought to become enlightened there are numerous who have become engrossed in the external message, the Exoteric as opposed to the Esoteric. Messages passed down become distorted or given self-interest driven meaning, but the bearers, the enlightened God realised sages, saint and prophets, remain eternal.

Endless permutations have been delved in to develop codes of practice, rituals and rules that are supposed to bestow some benefit, some purity, and some sort of credit rating for heavenly rewards. As a result the real world of human nature has been rejected. To become Enlightened, (so they say), one must become holy pure, and especially moral. Anything but human. Yet it is the acceptance of all states of being that is enlightenment. The understanding of what human being-ness is can be is the state of Divinity. It's here and now!

The individual who is struggling to avoid all the anti-enlightenment traps cannot easily succeed. The way is made possible by the presence of already enlightened ones whose company is the means. The bearer of the message of enlightenment, is the vision in human form of the desired state that is sought after by the earnest spiritual seeker. This one appears as the Grace for such a seeker who is already prepared to give up the search and the struggle. The surrender is the turning point, with the acceptance fully of the human form that is a true teacher, the Sat Guru. This process is acceptance of one's own native state of higher being, as the spark of recognition (of the natural state), that has jumped across to the student seeker. By all means have a "dead teacher" or a Higher Power outside of oneself, if that works. There is no Happy God in the clouds, (with a long beard of course). It's you, everyone else, and the whole of what you experience.

Be aware that the living human Guru is a representation of the Tantric way. This is because the form used is human. (And we know what humans are like). The characteristics, activities and behaviour of such an enlightened teacher can, and will be very ordinary, (as we all are at face value). Very typical of behaviour as of any other human. Even then a tendency has been to form cults around spiritual teachers, elevate them, and put them on a pedestal.

The purpose should be to show Divinity in human form, and make possible Divinity for the human species, inclusive of all his or her human frailties. Such a way, or path, avoids endless problems with trying to tame a human body full of strange thoughts as well as actions. We are full greed, hate, lust and so forth. (Just scratch the surface). We have to leave all that behind yes, but we, remaining as the individualised ego-based personage, are not going to make it, without the transcendental change.

Simply accept, then understood, and then transcend, then transform. There is no forceful asceticism, no strident moral posturing, (whilst desires are suppressed yet not destroyed). No religious crusading.

The "I'm holier than thou syndrome" is a recipe for war and chaos. The path of the enlightened teacher is the way of accepting the face of the Divine, and the ensuing transformation, whilst simply allowing that to support naturally one's own native state, until all the searching and seeking falls away.

If necessary accept the message and ignore the human frailties.

I can't get no Satisfaction!

Satisfaction is a strange entity. It seems to be an illusory state, an idea that changes shape of form according to the beholder. What is satisfaction for one is anthemia for another. Having a true ultimate endless unchanging satisfaction does not seem to be the position and experience of human life. It seems this way because of the immitigable fact of death. There can be no endless interminable bliss of joy in something that is just some temporary state that ends. Not only ends but sometimes abruptly unpleasantly and painfully. This is the human condition.

Most people acknowledge death as fact, although significant numbers avoid this issue any way they can, or bury their heads in the sand. Some people acknowledge that as far as their own death goes, they may not live to die peacefully in bed. Even so, deadly conditions such as cancer have been "corralled" to some extent. Thus, there may be more hope and more possibility of some sort of remission, pain relief and support from various services. This can give a better sense of control over a feelings and practical issues, and even some serenity during the death process. Nevertheless, the issue of death remains one that is and has been addressed in great depth by the spiritual guidance resources available, before and now.

However, the facts are that, although we live in an age of technological advance, death by technology is becoming increasingly common. Manmade catastrophes, road accidents, and a long list of other options. Trains, industrial, nuclear power, and even the mundane, like electric toasters! Add to the list some more exotic possibilities as those yet to be invented, yet to come, such as in genetic and Artificial Intelligence. This A.I. may not only take away jobs, but also do things like produce weapons that we can't even dream about!

Satisfaction seems to be a spiritual experience reach inwards as a heartfelt energy, encompassing metaphysical, gnostic, and (so they say), religious awakening. Wellbeing, without necessarily joyfulness, can be related to your choices, regarding what directions in life are taken, what ideals and morals are upheld, and what a belief system is doing for life stability. That may be satisfaction enough, but is it the Real Deal?

True inner satisfaction, with innate Bliss, is a normal birth right of our essentially Divine purpose and nature. Religious people will say of course that you must have an outer personal God, or that the idea of God residing in me and you is blasphemy! Burning at the stake was the historical cure for such aberration of thought!

There seems to be one problem or rather one large problem. It seems that virtually no human being is in this space, experiencing unalloyed bliss and satisfaction in life.

There are a few who seem to be practicing and demonstrating a life of divine awareness and who do emanate such a powerful force of constant bliss and knowledge. Especially in my travels in India I met a few such beings who for me were as realised and enlightened as it seems possible to be. Such beings have been described further this or other books. Until attainment of such an elevated stage, the Divine Self which is one's own two native state, is bound by the individual ego self. Bound by its own machinations, and psycho emotional tendencies.

Simply accept the nature of the Soul to be Divine, to be transcendental, and the giver of supreme satisfaction, when realised. This is Sat, Chit, Ananda, as previously described in writings. Truth, Knowledge, Bliss. Not just the true nature of all existence but including all religions and spirituality. This state of Being is without need of any human consolation or diversion, through the awareness of the individual soul as one with the universal soul. Certainly not a concept dependent on any religious belief.

Such an awareness can only be a direct experience, as otherwise it is just another philosophical idea or belief. This self-realisation is attainable. So the concept of having total satisfaction in life is also attainable. This is the Buddhist Nirvana or the Hindu moksha, but could also be seen from other angles, including the concept of total wellness. Can it be generated in therapy? Maybe not! Do modern Western scientific, psychiatric or psychological methods and concepts provide the goods? Or does the westernised adoption of Eastern philosophies and practices offer possibilities that work?

Questioning the truth of everything may lead to experimenting with different pathways, religions, therapies. This in turn may raise more questions and answers, as it could lead into another whole bunch of cul-de-sacs, consisting of various cults and sects. The whole field of religious and spiritual belief practice is fraught with power struggles, ideological clashes, or authority reactivity, which is really a pity and a diversion. It's a bit the same with a physically sick person who is being fought over by a horde of healers of different persuasion and techniques.

To move along a spiritual journey with any sense of stability can be a difficult process, and a struggle experience for years of a seeker's life. Religious movements of all sorts also have been seen as threats to the fabric or sanity of our materially orientated Society. Simultaneously the spiritual search comes up against one's own internal self-doubt driven barriers, plus the lure of addictions! Try giving up something such as chocolate or cigarettes. Does the craving usually go away in sympathy because you want to get healthy? Do the companies about to lose your custom feel happy?

So anyone just even trying something different from the life of the daily grind and suffering and conventional spiritual practice, is faced with a struggle, just to get started. You may be seen by your near and dear as being a bit of an idiot who needs to be better guided or even blocked and stopped! The establishment also seems to be in a peculiar opposition to any attempts at individual salvation done on one's own terms. The spiritual seeker who is practicing meditation and adds in a focus on the kundalini and chakra energies, may undergo an upheaval or a major change of bodily and mental stability. The spiritual journey does not lead pronto to some comfortable place in the sky, or a quick transfer to a land flowing with milk and honey.

It is essential to get the guidance one needs.

Shop around, be cautious, be ready to jump ship, and don't get swayed by the fundamentalists!

Having said all this from the "dungeon of doom and gloom", plunge in and abandoned all fear.

You are essentially Divine, and Divine Guidance is available as you call for it.

Have faith in your Deity, your Higher Power, your Sat Guru, or your Goddess.

The journey will occur anyway at some stage, and it is better to jump before you are pushed!

Tantra. Choose your poison becomes, "choose your nectar".

In the rat race to succeed and prosper, the stresses generated have given rise to a culture which seeks tranquility through medication, (hence tranquilizers). This includes the "poison of your choice", be it alcohol or drugs. Interestingly the spiritual seeker is faced similarly with multiple choices of how they wish to get "relief" from life. Now known well to the Western world are the choices of yoga, meditation and mindfulness. Even though these ways have come from the Orient, they seem through association with scientific research culture, to be in some ways devoid of any religious connection. Even so some Christians have said that yoga classes are not really suitable for Christians because they are from other beliefs. However, in general the public has not looked at their origins to closely. Nor have those who do a little yoga and meditation been seen as too interested in the complex religions that they have emanated from.

The "guru phenomena" from the 70s, and later, has, led to groups, sects and cults which though borrowing from Eastern religion, have now maintained more practical association with old European manners and customs. Vegetarianism stands to be one exception, as not a practice really that is connected to say Hinduism or Buddhism, even though historically India had a huge population of vegetarians.

Religion was as in the West in the Middle-Ages, just the foundation of all culture. Once a deep running interest in Eastern philosophy, but now tailored to Western need, is in way how as Tantra Yoga is perceived. Essentially Tantra leads to seek attainment of Liberation or Divine Realization through human experience, (which does of course include sex). This is as opposed to avoiding it, (life and sex), through monastic life. (In say, Thailand, the monks are still revered as "the holy ones", and not just any general public member). The scientific focused western individual, (or more bluntly, the materialistic one), is certainly very much enmeshed and interested in the outer world of senses meeting their sense objects. Hence Tantra suits this type of person because it is designed as a way of practicing spiritually through worldly experience. Although designed and promoted in the Indian sub-continent, Tantra never really found a major base of adherents there, as the "superior" spiritually tendency in India leant towards monasticism and renunciation of the world as the "proper" way to achieve holy status. (This is changing now, with the leaning towards more secular materialistic values). However, without the pure traditional aspects of Buddhism, there is tradition of a Tantric base that emanated from the area of Tibet.

In the West it is interesting that many of the Buddhist orders are Tibetan Tantric in origination. Some of the large groups of followers of Eastern gurus in recent times have also been clearly devoted as much to physical experience as to inward psychic ones.

Tantra is often seen as the "religion of sex". It is in a way, but is also the religion of food, money, relationships, searching for meaning in a material world, and basically anything to do with human experience. The word "tantra" means simply to "spread out", as opposed to the meditative or inward ways of other spiritual practices. Enjoyment of sense objects is a fundamental part of life, and it seeks to use that sensual experience as opposed to fighting or renouncing it. Tantra is extremely logical for a person who by nature finds it overly difficult, or impossible to adopt or adapt to an ascetic way in order to become Enlightened. Tantra as a way to Enlightenment, is through using the daily reality a front of us, not trying to avoid it.

Tantra seeks to use the everyday experience of sex, food, touch, taste, smell and so forth in way that is designed to both allow understanding and transcendence of them. (See also connections with kundalini, mantra, and the Goddess Shakti, as the prime Universal Force. There are deep practice connections where the world of experience is used to facilitate the spiritual journey!

Get with the Program!

There are always lots of questions regarding the spiritual journey and spiritual pathways.

We often do things based on fear rather than what will give us enlightenment or realization.

Do you want to survive at least, if not thrive?

A lot of life becomes based on culture, politics, and even religious "rules", rather than based on a search for the Meaning and the Truth of all life.

In life most problematic things can be sorted to some degree.

Even major health issues like depression and addiction can be addressed through therapy, rehabilitation, and even medication.

Family and relationship issues can be resolved, or at least we can get to a point of resolution where we know what cannot be changed.

Then life becomes about acceptance and the serenity prayer begins to make sense.

Always, however, the person who wishes to avoid pain also seeks pleasure in life.

Free choice will still take precedence.

So, regarding choice, we also have this concept of *karma*. We have suffering and pleasure, and success, and failure in proportion to our previous activities, and then our current activities create new karma.

This can be individual, but it can also be collective, as

we also tend to fit in with the cultural norms for our particular society and country, or religion.

In some places if we do not toe the line on religious matters we can be killed or jailed for blasphemy!

To move past all the structures is necessary to find the Realization and Enlightenment that exists beyond.

Then what we get is Knowing, and therefore the essence of the world is perceived very differently.

Then it becomes possible to change things radically, because we are in a place of understanding where we can be active in life, but based on Spiritual Truth to guide us. This is probably when we get into deep meditation, yoga and our specific spiritual pathways.

Then it's possible to see the Divine, not as a summary of our knowledge or some outcome of prayer practice, but as what is "All and Everything".

Indeed this can only be all or nothing.

God cannot be all of creation and not something within creation. Nothing can be excluded.

Light is required to see through the darkness though.

The teacher may be the Guru.

"Gu" stands for darkness and *"Ru"* stands for the piercer of the darkness, the bringer of light.

That is why we have teachers to bring light to our pathways until we no more need them. We don't need to put them on a pedestal, or become fanatics, as we just need a little light so we can get on our way. Thanks very much!

What we see in the light is very different from what we see in the dark.

In the light all is somewhat ok to live with. Sure, even the bad people!

Of course, how are you achieving this "level" is up to you. Religion of your choice or choose what you will as your pathway.

The information in this teaching is only "an example". If it has a use take what you will.

By all means your way may the only way and the only truth for you.

It's just normal human behavior to do things from

free-will/choice.

However, when you are really in the Light you will not need to judge others.

Neither their spiritual practice, nor their religion, nor their culture, nor their political beliefs-ever!

You will know who you are and what the Truth is of: *Life and the Universe*, and that the world around you, is an emanation of the Divine in its entirety.

You will then really understand what your purpose is and what the human body is all about.

However, if you deny some part of your life you won't be able to see the fullness of the Divine Energy, and part of you stays in darkness.

This goes down to the level of service, and how you treat your fellow human beings. How you deal with the homeless, the sick and the mentally unwell.

This is not about being like Jesus or the Buddha. You don't have to like anyone particularly. You don't have to make friends with everyone. But you do need to recognize the Divine in all, and in all people.

This way of being has always been present, and the great sages and seers, and incarnations have been on earth to help us to see the pathways, and sometimes to push us gently, (or a lot).

Nature sometimes pushes not so gently, as we see in the present chaos in the world and the potential for a lot of life loss. (Or even planet loss).

The principle remains the same. Remain in your Divine Center and the world around you, in any circumstance, will be seen by you as but emanation of the Divine Energy

When you see things that way you create also a whole new world that is by your very being, creating a light-filled place of serenity and peace.

This activity of your spiritual journey can even change the tendency of the world to engage in war and conflict!

OM GURU OM

The Challenge

Now as we continue the spiritual journey, we find ourselves in a place where we may not need all the same signposts, because we have arrived where we want to be, or we have found a way to know where we are going.

At this point we may well not need the references of culture, family, and work, to define ourselves.

This may seem scary, may feel like withdrawal, or a loss, but it is actually a new opportunity to have more, not less.

Before the Big Bang, "in the beginning there was the Word".

If you stay with the sacred sounds, you're connected with all the molecules in the universe and are enlightened as a realized human within the milieu that is life. Yes, there is suffering, pain, and struggle:

but that is life.

Realization is the acceptance of life as it is, as a Divine Creation at all times and for all purposes. We at all times are part of the Divine Creation, just as a drop of water is the same water as in the sea.

This is not a religion: this is just what could be considered normal!

Humans have added all the accoutrements of religions and spiritual pathways to the Divine Presence, which is the same for all, regardless of what human add to It. You can agree that there are multiple gods, different gods, and/or it's possible to have one "better" God than another, and so forth. (As well as being mono-theistic

So, the spiritual practice is being on a pathway that leaves behind the old and gets the understanding that the body is just: "compartments and bits and pieces". Separate seemingly from the Cosmic Reality, yet actually not separate.

Where humans have a major strength, it is in announcing ones essential "Divineness not divine-mess"!

With this strength it becomes possible to divert from, go around, go through, and go over: all the human weaknesses, including addictions, mental health problems, relationship distress, and physical sickness. Even financial distress, (or especially financial distress).

This is not a minor undertaking of course.

Turning everything upside down on its head, opens the individual to unlimited potential.

The ego still wants to have a sway and say, "no, no". This is my job, this is my partner, this is my car, etc. etc.

We can move above the level of identification and limitation and find the Truth and Reality.

We don't abandon reality, but rather work through it, with it, and understand it, such that it is not ones essential self that is in the way, but ones ego-based life.

So, it's not possible then to say that anyone is ultimately bad, or hard to say something is anything as other than a part of that One Unity. Self-centered judgment is usually based on ego preferences! In saying I am not part of the Divine, I will then need constant help, support, and opportunities to get what I can or grab in the struggle to survive. And I may or may not get this from this life ever!

Maybe initially this view of the all-enveloping Divine is just an idea of the moment, whilst starting on some spiritual path or religious pursuit. These "elevated" ideas, this kind of knowledge and experience don't usually arise of their own. Something happened to trigger this motivation. Then there can be incentive to follow the assistance of a suitable teacher or guru, or other contact that is more than "just human being". Maybe strong feelings of discomfort are initially engendered about such spiritual dimensions as expressed here. It is the nature of the ego to seek safety in what is known.

At some point however life stops being "what you do for yourself", and the Cosmic Will makes things happen, whether we want them or not. We see this in the chaos around in present times.

If we don't jump out of the burning house, we will go up in flames. (Unless we put out the fire).

If we don't see the winds of change blowing and except them, we will suffer simply by being dragged into change unwillingly.

It is a choice then take on board the teachings of the ancient sages and seers, the sacred and our True place in the universe, align with the divine sounds, or engage in spiritual practices innumerable. It's always as per individual choice, even if initially this is only an impulse to get a taste of some spiritual teachings and pathways.

Even religious "persuasions" may have a role to play!

Justifying the past.

It seems to be a normal tendency to look back and say, "oh I did that, why did I do that, what a mistake", or even, "how stupid of me".

In the deepest realized place, it is not necessary to have examination of what happened.

If you throw out the garbage, the rubbish, it's just going out, and it's not necessary to check every little bit in the rubbish bag.

Consciousness is the underlying substratum of "how it was, how it is, how it will be". Something else, anything else for me just does not have any great meaning.

Even so we may want to live in what is a bit of a museum and interpret things over and over.

Therefore, to move into the state of realization, is to be in a place which is essentially undefinable, and cannot be connected to by words and language. (Even though religions and spiritual teachings "have a go").

One's own Divinity is already in perfection, and as for

what happened and will happen, it's still within that Cosmic Consciousness.

We are what we think, and when we start think Divine, we start to move beyond "mere human". We become what we think.

It does not mean that the world does not exist. Some philosophers and spiritual practitioners call the world illusory. (Maya). That may be just another attempt to explain the inexplicable.

When we experience the Truth of existence, the true reality, we comprehend what I call: *Life and the Universe*.

In the universe we can enter into a nameless space in the ether of the cosmos around us. This is also within our hearts when we meditate. The Divine is not just out there, or not just some god sitting in the clouds growing his beard!

Ideas of God again are the product of history, many religions, and many thoughts of philosophers.

Some call it the great Buddhist Void, or *Shunya,* and in Post-Vedic times it was "Existence, Knowledge, Bliss". (*Sat, Chit, Ananda*)

The great sages, seers, and teachers say that we are in sync with the truth of God in terms of sound, (becoming form), and can go beyond sound also into the soundless etheric space. (The *Akasha*).

In any moment and time this present is what is available, what can be known, and this is where the mind can expand in mindfulness meditation to become united with the source of all, or one with the Cosmic Self.

It does not matter too much about a journey, as every experience can also be seen as part of the Divine Learning Experience, and be recognized as totally purposeful. (With no experience needing or any judgement to be added on).

When we accept who we are in Truth we claim our Divinity. We claim our Oneness with the Higher Power, the Divine Goddess. (Or God, if you insist).

When we do this we can also begin to demonstrate in our practical lives more than just survival. We move past fear, addictions, depression, anxiety, and whatever it is that troubles us as a human.

Again we accept those experiences of pain through mental struggles as part of Divine Learning.

But, we move beyond them!

If we continue to choose to deny our own Divinity, we are denying the Divine in all. We remain a human who wants God to fix us, or some other "version" to do so. (The incarnation, the Guru, the Buddha, the Jesus). We want to be fixed and stay human, really so that we don't have to take on the enormous responsibility incurred when we fully surrender to Truth.
Most religions will not give you permission!

To embody yourself in your true identity is heretic, and certainly you are not given permission, by most of society, to be "allowed" to realize your Divinity throughout your whole physical body.

Then it becomes required that you remain in fear. Fear because of separation. Where there is many there is no Unity. When we are one with the Cosmic Being we become fearless.

And, in fearlessness we lose our anxiety, sadness and our obsessions!

Chapter 4
The *Gunas* — What is happening?

The "Qualities" of Nature or *Life and the Universe*.

I try not to repeat too much the extensive use of Sanskrit words, which was after all focused around my spiritual practices as a monk in India.

There is however an interesting description in Sanskrit about three qualities or *Gunas* of nature.

If you are into healthy activities, healthy diet, and engaging in spiritual practice, our nature has some "purity. This is *Sattva Guna*. (*Sattva* means "pure").

If we are engaged in the world of pleasure seeking or engaging in life for material benefit mainly we are *Rajasic* and in *Rajo Guna*.

If we are living in darkness, addictions, suffering

deep mental health problems, we are *Tamasik* Stuck in *Tamo Guna*. In the darkness

Therefore, there are three qualities of nature, and three types of food, and three types of activities, and so on.

Have a guess which *Guna* you are sitting in!

A lot of us plough our way through this world through our respective careers, marriage, relationships, social experiences, hobbies, interests, and especially desires. So, Rajo Guna predominates.

In Sattva Guna meditation is spontaneous and does not necessarily involve sitting in a quiet room. However, it becomes also natural to enjoy contact with spiritually minded people, who also meditate, or have some devotional philosophy. The realized person doesn't feel the need to journey to anywhere on this plane or even to follow any rules that spiritual practice usually mandates.

Nevertheless, the qualities of nature still exist.

Going down dark roads and you're sick of it all? It means you're in Tamas mode

When we are in Sattvic mode we are pure, and we like activities with health giving outcomes, both mental and physical.

This means also we eat simple healthy food and avoid Rajasic food. (Think coffee here!). Alcohol is Rajasic, but alcoholic drinking is Tamasic, when it becomes destructive.

From a realized souls perspective, the Gunas act at all times but the soul is the witness of those activities. So from that perspective technically we can be Enlightened and yet behave in the mode of any of the Gunas. E.g., "the drunken master". (As described in some Tibetan texts. it's theoretical!).

Rajasic persons like the pleasures of life: good food and wine, with "life in the fast lane" a popular goal.

Then consequently we suffer physical problems from the minor, such as indigestion, to severe, such as heart attacks, money loss, addictions, and depression/anxiety.

We are high sometimes and depressed sometimes.

We rage and rant, fueled by desire, and aim for own personal gain.

If we are in Sattvic mode we cope with life in equipoise.

The Tamasic road is dark, and we may be deeply into addiction, but now at a painful level only.

Violent, stupid or destructive, become descriptor words.

In Sattvic mode though, we may not even be seeking self-realization or engaged spiritually as we maybe are just happy and satisfied enough, and we are lucky to have this personality.

Strangely I have felt more of an urge to turn to the spiritual side as a result of some destructive, negative, depressed, or addictive periods! However, it may be true that part of life's journey includes a good experience of all the Gunas.

Keystone phrases.

Firstly, let's take the word *enlightenment*

Delete!

Then the word *realization or self-realization*

Delete!

Why?

A lot of zeros have no value, but if the number one is place before the zeros then we have 1 million, (for six zeros).

I have a body I have a mind.

I have relationships, careers, and so forth plus my spiritual bit as the soul.

My spiritual beliefs may be giving me a sense of being enlightened but remember this word is not in favor in this essay.

We may have recovered or are in recovery from mental health, addictions, physical issues, relationship issues, career issues.

We can use the word "in recovery" because this is the case as long as we have a body and mind.

I am where I am now due to strong effort 's: searching and learning. My spiritual practices led me to a space, a Higher Room, from where I was able to connect with my strengths and resilience, with which I could achieve my recovered/recovery status.

We need a new word then which encompasses "perfection", that is spiritual, (and religious if you really need it), but also acknowledges worldly, physical and mental "perfection."

Perfection here is a sense of confidence, capability, and ability to resolve life issues as far as realistically possible, and to feel fully spiritually developed (or fully immersed in the spiritual journey).

It's a place where all the issues of "Life and the Universe" have been re-identified into the Divine Truth for the human in individual form. With the personality intact!

Fears are resolved and individuals can sit in their own Divine Space, higher power/room.

Technically then what happens is simply the ongoing experiences of life which happen automatically over the course of time, as karma outcomes.

That realistically enlightened individual no longer acts to get, make, achieve, but rather will experience, (the results of past actions).

Teaching or service to other may still take place as per one Deity inspired influence

The new phrase then is:

Practical Enlightenment. Also I like *Realistic Realization*

Now this is a sense of being, simply experiencing life, (as if the train ran out of fuel but keeps on roiling).

This is what is happening to one, around one, automatically as a result of past actions

It doesn't mean the person doesn't shower or eat etc. because these are also activities set up previously to perpetuate the life lived, and thus "roll" automatically.

It does not mean one doesn't go to work or doesn't remain in the marriage or other relationships.

Again these are set up and continue at their own pace under their own steam unless of course they spontaneously, naturally drop away.

There is no striving either to change things the way they are they are

It is as it is.

But there is no issue, no complaint, no fear, no anxiety, or regret.

This is *Practical Enlightenment and Realistic Enlightenment.*

Therefore, I write a reflection of what happened to me in my journey through life which was in its foundation a spiritual journey combined with, entwined with, the realities of life, relationships work, money, and whatever comes under the heading: *Life and the Universe.*

Surrender

There seems to be some idea that spiritual surrender is about giving up our attachments.

This seems more like acceptance, where we accept life "as it is" Then, we sit in our Divine knowledge and whatever happens is *Prarabdha*. (A Sanskrit word for the accumulated force of past karma). This is where a *Brahma Gyani* sits. (Knows themselves, as one with the Cosmic Soul, *Brahman*). Hence the word Gyana, which is knowledge of Brahman, the Cosmic Soul. (The individual soul is called the Atman, and this topic is written about in depth when the ancient philosophy of Vedanta was discussed in *Om Divine Grace*).

When you surrender spiritually, you stop making or seeking solutions to the uncontrollable. In the 12-step model its: "my life became uncontrollable". (Hence then the need to surrender to a Higher Power). To stop seeking solutions also seems to be about acceptance. Surrender is willful acceptance and yielding to a dominating force and its will.

Acceptance helps you accept the good and bad equally.

However, surrender also is to become aware of the Divine as oneself, with the Higher Power's energy *within*, and to accept it. It involves a shift in belief or approach to the spiritual journey, and is about "Who am I?"

Is this a catalyst for enlightenment?

Trust, and faith that there is a Divine Force seems to be a pre-requisite for surrender. "I believe that God will help me through this". This requires some awareness of options generated by the usual questioning that goes until a belief in the Divine co-exists with faith in your spiritual teachers.

Not just: What is this all about?

But also: What do I do (as service)?

The act of surrender requires some practical substance also. Mediation, prayer, chanting, using a mantra etc. What is the single most powerful tool you use on your spiritual journey? You can't think "I don't have to do anything else", and not do the practice required.

By turning your awareness away from normal activity and settling the mind, you can reconnect with your inner space. In the silent spaces beyond thoughts, you surrender to a Sound, the Cosmic Sound. Just as there is noise in life, so there is noise in realization. It very different though and can't be explained, only experienced.

You submerge your ego, which remains but is transformed, into identity as the Divine, where there is the bliss of Oneness. (When you can hear then the Cosmic Sound).

If all else fails, just pray for surrender. It doesn't matter who or what you pray to, it matters only that you are willing. The intention to surrender will allow its own release, and who knows, maybe there is an old man up there sitting in the clouds! (For me it's the Goddess, but I'm not saying my beliefs are any less "naïve")! Anything that helps with the letting go of fear and unending desire is worth a try.

Again, the small self, the individual "me," is not capable of dropping its own sense of ego, even though the Atman is intertwined with the Brahman. (Just as water is water, whether in a drop or in a sea). Maybe the "rock bottom" of the addict or a state of impasse, or "the darkest night", triggers some transcendence. It is a pity that it may have to occur this way! A realization "I simply cannot do it, can't win, can't complete, can't change the situation". Something has to change, even if is occurring within a state of mental disorder. Someone will come to attend to you even if temporarily, involuntary, as when mental health becomes life threatening.

If however, you trust the Divine then the Divine Grace leads from darkness to light.

When we agree to participate in the process of surrender to our Higher Power or place our lives in the hands of God then we are met by the Divine

Force.

The change occurs when there is willingness to access and seek the Truth.

This makes us available to be witnessed and to witness.

We can then stop hiding and leave the past shames and fears behind.

The Divine Self as the individual soul can then be healed by Divine Grace.

Maybe medication, therapy, rehabilitation, or other treatments will work.

Maybe

Or rather all the healing opportunities in the world may be helpful "to a point'. Maybe

The issue finally is about being at another level.

This is not just about praying to seek the god, the higher power, or ones deity.

It's about being in one's own Higher Power, being in the Divine Self and experiencing Divinity in human bodily form.

We have been claimed by a situation where we may live very fearful human lives, whilst at the same time seeking redemption, solutions to suffering within and without our personal lives.

There is a necessity, or a choice, or we are pushed to move "past the past". To release all of life in a higher way through the encounter with one's own Divine Self.

The rubbish or garbage is put out, and there is no need to check and go through it all. Just throw it out! Let it go to leave the darkness behind.

Freedom from self-condemnation, anger or righteous action, becomes grounded and light, and only then is the darkness absent.

Some would say that the material reality is an illusion.

The Sanskrit word for this is Maya, the delusional dreamlike transitory life experience.

The true Maya though is that we believe there is happiness all around us. In success, money, and even relationships.

The Buddha indicated that "all life is suffering"

Thus, life and free will at a high level seeks not to totally alleviate personal strife, but to see the Truth of life's journey as having an ultimate benefit for all. Cancer is not eliminated. Mental health disorders are not eliminated. Poverty is not eliminated. War is not eliminated.

We just don't participate from the same angle anymore, we have a radically different perspective and understanding of what is the universal Divine Consciousness.

Which cannot be in truth separate from anything or anyone.

Either this "consciousness" is homogeneous, or it doesn't exist for a benefit, (as it would not then be anything of spiritual value)!

The ending of delusion, the end of the chase of dragons and dreams, can be celebrated.

Accomplished by agreeing and participating in the spiritual journey, and that can be accomplished by being on a path of one's personal choice.

There are signposts, teachers, and guides to help us. Even that the parts of religion that have not been corrupted can serve a purpose on this journey.

It's all available if we seek it, but more than that it will only work if we let it.

That is where the challenge of surrender lives!

Acceptance

The problem with surrender is that there follows acceptance.

Our God, Higher Power or Divine has a plan with exactly what we need to be given when we need.

This seems scary!

What if it's not true!

What if I don't like what I get?

It's a bit like going to a restaurant having to eat what is placed in front of oneself, instead of ordering.

What if I get non-vegan?

Or fish?

The good thing is that confusing choices can be released. What do I do about my marriage? What do I do about my job?

The Divine ensures that each step is revealed to one who makes the surrender and waits.

Answers come with surety as the inner voice, which only makes good sense, is a true voice.

Thus, a word of warning. Those who are mental health professionals are well aware of the delusional content of the mind in states of sickness, when thoughts can be misleading, dangerous and life-threatening.

It may pay to check things out with a suitable professional person, guide, or therapist.

It's also a good idea to do so with a health professional if one is susceptible to unraveling, or is vulnerable to a mental health condition.

The issue is not really about what will happen to you, or what you will do, or how your five-year plan will work out. It's about sitting in a space where fear and anxiety about, *Life and the Universe* is alleviated.

Of course we desire, we want great things, and that lottery win.

Being in the Divine place is not about forceful relinquishing of our desires or even addictions.

It's about being in a space where it is natural to accept the fullness of life "as it is", and thus the needs and wants disperse, vanish or become irrelevant.

Gratefulness for what we have not what we haven't

got.

Acceptance is that there is enough, and I can share fully what I have got.

I don't have to win to the detriment of others. (Maybe sport is different).

Being one with the Divine Self will enable outcomes of benefit without or beyond limitation.

Far greater things can happen.

There still will be in counters in life that confuse, and cause fear and anxiety but again the Divine Design is that we learn.

Everything is included as part of the spiritual journey.

Thus desire can be re-purposed and re-understood, as something to not fight against, but something that purposely placed in the correct position in the scheme of things.

Chapter 5
Divine Grace!

There is possibly no need for Divine Grace.

If we could all achieve Nirvana, salvation, enlightenment, through our own normal natural efforts then we might only need the help of a few teachers or gurus.

There is some agreement that as humans we are in some sort of a mess, that we need to get out of this, whether this is seen as be freedom from sin and placement in heaven, or breaking the bonds of ignorance and preventing future reincarnations. Or some other perspective.

Most religions seem to have a view that the Divine is actually within, as well as without. Usually, the heart is designated the place for it all to happen.

This view is also the foundation of the Vedanta philosophy, where it is proclaimed that additionally this natural state is what drives the urge to attain salvation.

In this philosophy the sinner and the saint, good and bad, rich and poor, are equal in terms of being part of the Cosmic Consciousness, (the Brahman), expressed as the individual soul, (the Atman).

In summary all religions are clear that we can be saved in some form and get into a kingdom of some form of God enveloped "space" or presence. Again the essence is within our souls and probably associated with the heart area.

This may seem like that is all about being totally self-responsible, and about trying one's best to do good deeds, serve others, and pray to one's Deity. Where from then comes this closely intertwined doctrine of Grace, inseparable from the search and the seeker? Especially when grace seems to render self-responsibility nil and void at times.

Grace is pretty certainly not something that stands out as completely separate, but then again why is it placed sometimes as the ultimate, "out there somewhere". Also, it is fairly often proposed as being the only way to achieve liberation.

The Buddha did not seem to speak much of Divine Grace, whereas in the worlds of other religions, with scriptural announcements about being chosen through Grace seem fairly prominent.

It seems then one can believe that "I have attained what I have by my own struggles", as long as one then says "my struggles got me nowhere and it was the Divine Grace that illuminated me".

A bit confusing perhaps if we have to wait until it flows "down". (Grace that is).

What's the point of doing anything?

And how come some can get it another does not?

Perhaps the problem lies with promoting either human type attributes to a personal Being or a computer type vagueness that mostly equates karma with just outcomes. "As you sow so ye shall reap".

It's perhaps a bit of a leap to think about the Divine Grace as belonging in the field of an impersonality, or atheistic type belief, as surely it can't be a robot like evolutionary "energy"? (Created only by the developing or evolving human mind).

Another way around any conundrum exposed, is to understand that we are covered in ignorance due to the presence of Maya, the "illusory" nature of the world. Lost in a recurrence of our dream, we are just in our ignorance, and we just can't see the Truth. (Groundhog Day)?

That ignorance is our normal self, just our usual everyday personality based ego.

When we choose to surrender the ego, we get the Grace.

Easy on paper!

The Grace is there, you have just got to get hold of it,

or rather not get hold of it, but position yourself where it flows and be in the stream.

This logically leads to doing an activity that makes things happen and allows Grace to flow.

Do some prayers, try a mantra, and learn to meditate.

Next step is getting some discipline! What about those addictions, and who knows, even obsessive behaviors and attitudes! Get a program which is monitored and supported by someone who knows the way and the ropes. Become: "resting in the hands of the counsellor, guru, or sponsor".

What If the ego says: "no I can't do it I'm just a hopeless drunk", "my depression is too deep" am unable to escape an unhappy marriage", or I'm just plain too scared, (to change)? Then perhaps it is time to accept the loss of power of the ego and surrender to receive the Divine Grace. Fix your mind on God your Higher Power or Deity.

What about the atheist?

There will be an alternative way if you look. Just as if you go vegan gluten-free or FOD-map diet, you will find something to meet your nutritional needs. (I am a bit facetious about the atheist bit-sorry)

We still remain bound to the law of action, bound to death, (and taxes), but karma is not our master. Choose the Divine Master and keep trying because when you kind of give up, that's when your ego gets weaker.

Well, what about my marriage, children, and career? Desire for a new car, kitchen, or overseas travel? Well do you like the bondage-based years, and years of life and death. Is this freedom for you?

If so carry on!

If not, there may not be another way. (Other than Divine Grace).

Alternatively, if you are already Divine, you are already free. It is your own true nature. Just remove the veil of ignorance, generated through worldly obsessions.

Human beings with intelligence may reflect that something is missing, without understanding the spiritual aspect necessarily, let alone the meaning of *Life and the Universe.*

You don't have to do it anything really arduous, you don't have to "retrain", and you don't have to like people, or be liked.

Think about getting the life that's going to be source of your Eternal Bliss.

Ramifications for me.

Previous writings have covered some issues regarding both Grace and spiritual practice using mainly Vedanta based philosophy that could be seen by Western philosophy as Gnostic.

Vedanta says *Aham Brahma Asmi.* I am the Divine or Cosmic Consciousness and the world is Maya. (Illusory). This can be seen as religion without a God, and has similarities to Buddhism, which evolved in India post Upanishads. (The scriptures defining Vedanta, which were written at a later stage of the

Vedas. (Veda and anta=Vedanta).

Yet the other core component of my spiritual practice has been the worship of the Goddess as my personal Deity, which in practice has entailed engaging in Kundalini Yoga. This for me is working with the centers of the body, the chakras, through which the kundalini passes as it arises from the base of the spine.

This practice is also about Shakti, the Divine Goddess energy, which can be invoked using mantas, especially "seed" mantras. (Described in depth in my book *Om Divine Grace*).

So, in some respects this combines both a personal deity with an impersonal deity and some "scientific" practice of working with bodily centers using the Yogas of meditation, mantra and yoga postures.

This may seem contradictory but has been in common practice from ancient times as per the writing of the sages and seers in India.

For the last year or so The Guides have been my gurus for the Gnostic part of my practice. Previously

I had human gurus that guided my practice as a monk and into later years. Also I have been guided or helped by a number of counsellors and therapists, in regard to psychological mental components.

The Guides speak through their writing as channeled directly through the books of Paul Selig. Paul says he only channels the words, and they come through, entirely without any addition or change or editing. The words that come across sound very much like my philosophy of the Vedanta, placed into much more modern terminology and perspective.

The Guides say we are all divine, we all live in a divine world that is undifferentiated in the sense that this perspective/belief is for everybody. All people have equal opportunity as they are all by birthright Divine beings, in their bodies and human lives. This is way more accessible than Vedanta which was really the domain of sannyasins and swamis initially in India. It is still often seen as a philosophy in the domain of renunciation and monastic leanings.

The goal the Guides propose is to stay or live in the Higher Rooms where one lives as one's higher self, which then allows all the answers to life questions to flow spontaneously. Then one's way of living automatically changes to one of living in the light, and one gets out of the darkness. Two key things for me led to me continue with readings of, six books in the series. Firstly, the goal is to be free of fear, totally and unconditionally, as when one is in the light in the darkness doesn't exist. As I have struggled at times in my life with depression, and anxiety (and therefore fear), therefore this has been my goal. (Even probably if I am honest, I suffered all these issues when I was a monk in India for those ten years). Secondly, I see the teachings as being completely open to anyone at any stage, without any necessary background. No previous knowledge. My time as a monk counts for nothing, my spiritual practice today to counts for nothing! Unless I make the free choice of surrender to the purpose of living in the Higher Rooms, and unconditionally accept my birthright to be a Divine being. (Under all circumstances).

I still do this also through my devotion to the Goddess alongside my monotheistic or non-dualist philosophic practice. The mantras are the activity, and these refer to specific goddess forms, (of the one Divine Shakti). As they are directed to specific chakras in the body, this repetition of mantras purifies and bring light to the human realm. They also work subtly on mental health issues, addictions and obsessions.

It is also a surrendering process. That is to leave it up to the Goddess or rather give it over to the Goddess. This can be replicated of course in whatever one's pathway or religion is, and as I am multi-faith I have absolutely no issue whatsoever with doing the same process through any religion or any spiritual practice. I don't have any issue or energy to discuss the benefits of one way or another, and I am simply not interested in debating my religion/s, (or politics). It is irrelevant, get on with the job, and attain enlightenment and realization.

Life events can be seen as an action directed by a force, based on which choice is made by the individual. Such choices, and then endeavors, range from choosing a totally materialistic or even animalistic lifestyle, to choosing a spiritual one, with all manner of variation in between.

The concept of destiny does not make me fatalistic,

rather more optimistic, cheerful and serene, due to knowing the true role of the outcome of that destiny. Destiny is my self-responsibility, and what happens is a function of the cosmic laws. Because I believe and feel the central Divinity of the Cosmos, I accept the pain as well as the pleasure of life equally and with equanimity, (because all experience is part of that Divinity).

I discovered that we all walk towards our Nirvana, and simply the ability of the world is to provide the necessary learnings. We can sit back when we see life "as it is and ourselves as we are". This does not cure or even deny room for change or personal growth. Just that one is able to work, without being affected dramatically by success or failure. Also, that any objective is already present as the perfect Self (The *Atman as one with Brahman*). The journey, the effort is also the goal. Do you live in terms of being self-realized, when what we want is already achieved, and anything else is also certainly achievable? (Within the realm of the dream Maya).

> *The True Self within is so near and yet so hard to find. All the yogis and gurus, they*

must recommend you ask the question:

Who am I?

Also seek the guru within as well as without. The Vedanta teachers say that when we ask ourselves, who am I, we are trying to find out what the true nature of the "I" is. Not mind, not body, but an unchanging entity, that remains constant through childhood to old age. It is the self within the Atman which is the same substance as the Cosmic Soul. All the teachers of this way point out not only the importance of the guru, but also of the Deity that one surrenders to.

I have realized that the minds activities are transient and fickle, and the light of yogic awareness burns steadily behind the mental screens. We reach the transcendental through the awareness of the light. Through our deepest subconscious, we can return to our chosen life of being one with Divinity flowing down to all levels of our human endeavor.

My years long ago in isolated huts and villages, gave me time and space to consolidate a core foundation Awareness. However, I came to realize one part only of my spiritual journey, which was of a reclusive isolative nature. That I was 50% complete or 50% incomplete! It did take me another forty years to resolve the rest.

The underlying and sometimes automatic subconscious thread of devotion to God still worked for me to enable a Grace that made practical the therapy, recovery, mental wellness, and strength or fortitude. The Western world and my ordinary existence of family, work, and finances has enabled me to understand how the esoteric Eastern based philosophy of Shakti is providing true understanding or spirituality. It's at all levels, through all cultures, and also props up the formless non-dual concepts of Vedanta enabling it to be, not just for monks, as traditionally it had been.

The Guides words have made it very clear to me that this "I am Divine', is for the present times for all. This is what we need now in what is a chaotic world of darkness. I had never seen my divine Shakti in a concrete vision but have felt the presence for a long time of a male spirit that has guided me or at least supported me. This personal presence completely resonated in agreement with what the Guides were saying, and I could re identify with elements of my "monk person" that I had held for so many years in India.

I made my choices and then sat back unable to *process Life and the Universe.* My life was unmanageable at times, and that is when the Divine has come down in the form of Grace. And this is spirit guidance. It's a surrender thing!

Transactions of ego in the matters of psychosexual, and romantic leanings after I left India, required of me to accept any mental discomfort experienced. That meant that the type of existence I continued with for many years thereafter submerged my spiritual journey into a mode of survival. I forgot any kudos I had gleaned as an ex-holy man. I think though I had to become a humble-man not a holy-man.

My guru in India, Swami Muktananda, was somewhat scathing when I turned up to his *ashram* in my robes speaking Hindi and looking like a Swami. He said in about two sentences: "you're always going to be English, no matter how Indian or Hindu you try to be. And what's wrong with Christianity"? I did not really except he had said those words. I pretended he hadn't. It took me a long time to see what he said was absolutely true.

The work of the Divine Goddess is this spinning of us into the web of Maya, seemingly on the surface.

Then to trip us into mundane activities, but really to eventually liberate, as the Divine works happen in the world, and not in some cave or monastery.

We are led to *Practical Enlightenment or Realistic Realization* eventually, as long as we are "on the pathway". We are all full of subconscious material relating to needs and desires but need to experience life through the physical persona in order to transcend the ego. Of course, free will and choice is involved, and I had to make a choice to surrender to the Higher Power, even if it was born of desperation.

The mantras that I repeat as part of my spiritual way led my individual self into an awareness of Universal Self, expressed as the Cosmic Sound. Eventually this sound can be experienced beyond meditation and bought right down through the chakras of the body to the toes and into all aspects of my life, "out there". Life and the Universe

With attraction to the Divine comes a natural

tendency to serve others, even if one is still a bit driven at times by excessive, obsessive, or pleasure-seeking type common human behaviors. I can see the goodness in the mistakes I made, but now I can say it's no longer about mistakes, they are just enriching experiences. I prefer to say: learning experiences.

Although I feel and talk of the Divine Spirit, it is also useful to place it in life experiences in terms of mental wellness, addictive behaviors, and pleasure seeking lifestyles. (All the baggage that goes with normal human behaviors out there). The real need is to remain focused on the goal of coming to the Divine awareness, and then realize the inner true guru that you know you are in essence.

Your guides: they are you and have purpose as separate, only to take you to awareness of the Truth, which coincides with the loss of the lower self through transcendence of your ego tendencies. Then you don't need gurus, you are the Guru!

This is the wakening of the day of the light. Whatever religion or spiritual pathway has got you so far. The purifying benefits in terms of ego transcendence leads to dimming or disappearance of the psycho emotional and addictive tendencies that cause so much havoc in so-called civilized society.

Because I see the Universal Spirit as manifesting through a power of the Shakti or Goddess creative Maya, I accept that the energy of Shakti has to be brought into real life. I see the need to deal with and understand this energy as essentially a female aspect of Divinity.

The marble form of the idol in the temple is a means to help with spiritual practice. It is not worship of a piece of marble, rather a useful means of purifying a psycho emotional mental deficit, and an activity done with a view to developing concentration and awareness. The purpose of any external devotion still is that the true nature of one's Divine self becomes self-evident into all levels of one's human form and existence.

The Goddess then represents both Maya in the whole world of human suffering, searching and pleasure seeking, and she also represents the link back to the Universal Being, which is formless, pervasive Cosmic Consciousness. Some people call it God. The Goddess is the energy represented by the Kundalini Force, which rises up the spine with the human awakening, to break through at the crown of the head, so as to allow the liberation of the soul.

The Goddess is also the focus of the Tantric way that includes the world in worship. Instead of exclusion, there is inclusion of "money food and sex". (Which needs to be dealt with appropriately). The Goddess is the link for me. A means of transferring human identity to Divine identity and to allowing the understanding of what my gurus and guides are talking about.

Now my awareness is of no religion, or even no spiritual belief that I have to defend. I do not have to follow any path, but I am simply aware of my own choices in this matter. I have opened up to any religious or spiritual experience that helps and accept the need for the many forms that religion and spirituality take.

Fear and pain

So, it's all Maya! Illusory like a transient dream ending in death.

Scientists will talk about the function of molecules constantly re-arranging themselves to form things, including humans.

Within that video, film, play of whatever it is going on, or however you perceive or describe it, is the process of one's thoughts and understandings about *Life and the Universe.*

"I am depressed. I am an addict. "I am a powerful leader", etc.

Maybe there is no problem with just accepting that I am a Divine being really, and life is just a sideshow, which is ultimately totally illusory.

Except for pain!

Pain and suffering makes all the theory irrelevant and can make all our spiritual or religious and therapeutic endeavors almost seem pointless.

This is the pain of life the Buddha talked about: "all life is suffering".

Whatever and wherever the journey or pathway to freedom, one thing is clear,

There is suffering when there is duality.

Where there is another there is fear.

Life is driven by an underlying fear.

Fear of death, of suffering or of life itself, and fear of God.

In the Divine Soul, there is no fear, because fear is just a human creation, the outcome of being engaged in in the human condition, and excepting the separation from the encompassing universe, whilst not recognizing Divinity, either as one Deity or as the impersonal Cosmic Consciousness.

There is a line of queuing thoughts that like to give fear permission to exist in oneself.

However, it's not possible to just say fear: "you're out of here".

In positive visualizations, however well-meaning, deeming that I am pain-free, just doesn't work.

We need something that works to enable the transcendence of this Maya.

We have to replace it with Truth.

Know the type of visualization that already has cognition of ourselves as potentially Divine.

Well possibly it takes time!

We know there are some who have amazing visions such as of Mary, Mother of God, described as happening in Medjugorje, or descriptions of someone getting a fantastic vision being reborn in a eureka moment, or having some other transformative experience.

A problem occurs for most of us, because that's not how it works for most of us, and that's not how it happens.

Also present is often this idea that enlightenment equals: "you are getting what you want, being happy all day and night, and can sort out anything". In Buddhism and Hinduism there are fierce goddesses, depicted in temple icons as cutting off human heads and drinking their blood.

They are the forces of destruction and epitomize the nature of this cosmic reality, that in error some religions seek to minimize. "Oh no our God is not nasty, He's kind and loving".

To worship destruction and darkness in any way seems counterproductive perhaps to the general Western mind, but to many in the East, it is very much this God as Destroyer that is sought to gain safety and security.

To have enlightenment, the dark side that must be something understood, and life as it is in its grossness, transcended or transmuted. This is *Alchemy*, as at one and the same time being able to transcend and enjoy the true spiritual meaning of *anything* that lies here and now and beyond. Thus the chaos makes sense. Thus, the pandemics make sense. Thus, even all the wars of history make sense!

This is also about encountering your true self, which seems covered in the fear and the suffering. The human ego is in a position to overcome. Transferred beyond, though, or under. Here lies surrender and acceptance, which is generated through spiritual practice and selfless actions. Knowing the true self would lead also to a space where each moment will bring whatever experience we need to when they are needed.

This life as lived, is also the learning journey, even if yet there is no spiritual inclination.

So, if one cannot understand the purpose of pain, dig a little deeper!

Then one can understand, pain, death, world chaos, and drill right down to the minutia of personal life.

Then it's no longer a question of shall I divorce, resign, run!

The answers are set up there in what has become instant participation in the vibration of Truth, which illuminates the darkness.

If spiritual progress is limited due to limited action, then perhaps only small corners of the darkroom will be lit up. Thus, fear will still be on the agenda. Although it will still have learning purpose.

The process is about release, ultimately from all the darkness.

Thus, we return in circle to the beginning of the discussion regarding surrender and acceptance.

What really goes on?

What goes on outside, but taken in through our eyes, thoughts, and are senses?

Thought sees "happenings" as something to hold on to and maintain.

It seems that life has a lot of things that we want or positions we want to attain.

Some of it we can touch, talk to, or directly experience through senses, but of course it eventually disappears or vanishes, or changes.

More often we see what we want, but we don't get it.

The other prospect is that we get or use what we like and want, and then become addicted to substances or behaviors, which then of course lose their power to pleasure.

So perhaps it will be better for all of us, if we just stay out of off the roads. Living in caves and just pass the time. That way we stay out of trouble!

If this does not make sense, then what does make sense?

There must be something, some way of living that makes sense in our world, and to our spiritual being as in leading to something super-special.

Religion may have some answers, and historically has done the job quite well for a lot of people

However perhaps modern life views of religion are adding up to finding out that you have a copy of Picasso, a fake! What about enjoying something, say black and white TV, (which is what I had as a child), and then discovering there is color TV!

Religion now does not seem to provide the answers to a lot of people in the Western world. In the Eastern worlds, religion is still a foundation of a culturally based society, but that also is changing quite rapidly now we have instant worldwide Google, Facebook, and YouTube. As we know, being in the world, even if our culture is still solid, does not automatically resolve some fundamental questions.

Who am I? What am I? What is my purpose?

Purpose

Perhaps having a purpose is not all it's made out to be.

Certainly, sometimes it seems there is no purpose at all, to anything.

But other times the sun is shining and all is well.

Another time a person may have deep faith, but a fundamentalist faith can be akin to burying one's head in the sand.

However, if that's what works what's wrong with that? Then all is well also!

It seems necessary in life to bring in mechanical means to alleviate suffering.

An illustration of this is taking medication for physical or mental health problems. We "forcefully" try to resolve the issue. This quite often is reasonably successful, otherwise people would not bother going to doctors or psychiatrists.

In the spiritual world or in the mental health world, there are other things we can do: activities to participate in. At one level there are talking therapies. We can try to heal through counselling psychoanalytical methods, or with practical efforts, such as using sensory modulation techniques to alleviate anxiety. Physical relaxation methods practice controlling the breath, listening to soothing music, or practicing some mindfulness type exercise.

If we go further still, then there are other things we may do.

We are then in the realm of prayer, using liturgical hymns, or using mantras. Or on a more physical level, some devotional worship, as for instance performed in temples.

We are almost trying to force God to come to the party.

We want to make it happen.

Why do we do this?

Why should it work?

Presumably there is some underlying understanding that must come from within us, in order for us to hold the expectation that some form of salvation occurs this way.

Indeed, all the teachers in the spiritual sphere will undoubtable mention as some component of their teaching that the Divine is within.

My guru said that the guru is also actually within. So some say when you find the Buddha tell him to go away, (as you don't then need the guru in form).

In other words, you're done, finished you've got it, and you've got what it needs.

Except this is just the beginning!

Then you need to expose yourself to the Devine Grace through your spiritual practice again and again until there is no more "again".

And then what life is still goes on. There is still the mortgage, to pay the pets to feed. Then what is just left is the suffering of the moment, the being in the body here now, which is not really a comfortable place by any measure,

The tummy rumbles, the nose itches, it's too hot or too cold, and we are always subject to hunger and thirst, plus the need for sleep in a place to sleep safely. Life is pretty dangerous, and it can be extremely dangerous. A matter of just survival for so many billions of people.

So this daily practice is what gives us the moment-to-moment relief (from our suffering), and this is where we can thrive instead of survive.

By this time, we will have formed a connection with our Deity, with our spiritual pathway, and understand the place of our particular religious beliefs in the whole picture.

By this time we should not be saying there is anything to fix nor anything to make different!

We should be now in the moment, being present, and if we are not really feeling it we should be using all the spiritual practice tools at our disposal. Prayer, mantra, meditation, or other means

Then there is no excuse, only self-responsibility. There is only the requirement to do what is needed moment to moment and "get on with it".

Deal with it, function and provide solutions, as far as one can. Beyond that we are at the mercy of our God!

Tara inspired 1

It would be nice to live a life that is easy without pain and without fear. Maybe possible for some to some degree. If we read the news, look around us, and possibly look at our own lives, we will see that this is not the case for the vast majority of people for the vast majority of the time.

From a spiritual perspective: *Life and Universe* is a learning experience for every moment or every breath.

Fear is a natural part of life since caveman times, when the fight or flight response was essential for survival. Now fear seems like a substratum, the foundation of our daily lives, and something that's happening all the time, including and up to, the fear of death. We do a lot of things both for our survival and because we are fearful about what might happen to us if we don't do certain things.

The spiritual teachers or Guides tell us that we are Divine beings, and in our Divine consciousness we are naturally free from fear. This does not translate into reality and probably never will if we are honest! Alright, reality itself may be seen as an illusion without permanence, it's a philosophy idea that for most of us, still does not translate into something spiritually meaningful or lived experience.

It will be helpful to be centered and focused within one's heart with solidarity with the level where you find a light that shines and inspires. This is where fear does not exist, and this translates or rather transforms the negative or dark energy in our lives. It will not just go away! It needs to be transmuted as in an alchemical process, and this may not happen in a "flash of light". (As in "I have seen the light"). Anything towards helping us to deal with fears, anxieties and depressions, will also help alleviate our core fear, and yes for some with clinical levels of depression/anxiety, medication may have benefits!

Cancer and other physical illnesses also will not just go away, just because we think we will, or may, take them out of existence. Again, there are those who have been "miraculously" cured, and those who have received great medical benefits.

But it is *Insane and fantasy thinking* to start putting any kind of outcomes in place, as the *guaranteed benefit* of any spiritual practice, positive thinking, or therapeutic healing etc. This is all ego territory, and the earnest spiritual practitioner should stay focused on what the real outcome of practice is. (Hopefully better self-surrender, better service of others, and a natural "high" based on love towards all life).

So, when we say, according to the Gnostic type philosophies, that I am the Cosmic Consciousness, or at least a Divine being, we are in psychological terms creating positivity and outlines or sketches for our individual souls to "feel into" the Cosmic Soul, who is free from all blemishes. (And fear, disease and pain). That is if we don't muddy the waters with our ego expectations.

The purpose or the agenda of the Truth is self-realization, not freedom from being human or experiencing what it is to be human. Human experience still goes on even for the so-called realized person, because of the cumulative effects of past karma. This experience of remaining in the body and experiencing spiritual resonance with Truth while still having work, family, physical elements, fear and anxiety, is part and parcel of this thing called:

Realistic Realization or Practical Enlightenment.

Accumulated effects and continuing friction from past actions are transmuted by the self-realized soul, who is unafraid, and doesn't worry about anything, because of Being in Truth. (Also, nothing is seen as "real" from a permanency perspective, including the body and mind).

To get to this position requires usually some additional activities on the spiritual journey, (other than a pure philosophical stance). This is the case to even just enhance the pace of the spiritual journey, or even to ensure the spiritual journey actually has some practical traction. This is where additional support from one's personal Deity comes into play. Religion has benefits for some!

I my case it's the Goddess who is available to smooth this process, and I dedicate this section to Tara the Tibetan Goddess. (Available in Hinduism also)!

This journey can be expedited in a very physical sense. That is to say one's anxieties and fears, can be addressed very front on, very much in the moment, by having oneness with the power and the Grace of the Goddess. (Through prayer and meditation).

Of course, he or she may do it through the Christ, Krishna, Buddha, or other. Your choice!

The point is there is a need for a personal God to assist in the understanding of a Cosmic Divine energy which is beyond all thought and speech. Therefore, it becomes necessary to be really practical, and except the Divine in whatever form or through whatever process that works to free oneself. There can be no space for judgement of anyone, for as you damn others, so that damnation returns to you.

Do unto others as you would do to yourself.

(So simple but to really do this, seems elusive).

We have first to get into a place of seeing, and feeling the essential unity of the universe, and have the tools to be able to do this sort of thing. As simple human beings we may be lost in our addictions, depressions and anxieties. We may need a whole raft of support type activities around us. Along with our "highest point" philosophy and claim of Self Divinity we may need some medication for whatever ails us also!

From a non-dual perspective the world is an idea, just a result of thought activity, just an illusion with transient nature. You make things how they are by how you think. The human desires then acts, then then achieves, (or fails). In Divinity one does not act and if any actions take place, it is only the qualities of nature moving. These qualities of nature, (the Gunas), have already been written about. They range from the pure to the filthy, the dark and deprived, to the place of light and selflessness.

So, the spiritual journey requires that we don't give away our agenda of humanity, but we do give away the small individual soul, and the agenda that is based on darkness. An ego-based darkness which is full of, not just fear and anxiety, but also hatred, self-serving and the historical mankind starting point for: "divide and conquer". (Historically also: "loot, rape and pillage")!

Although the qualities of nature remain in control of the universe, we retain our self-responsibility for self-determination and choice. A choice to be at the highest level of Being, is claimed by the highest level of practicing spiritually. Focused with rigor and honesty, meditating in that state in the form of the form of God "as you understand Him/Her".

Without operating from one's own perceived or actual state of depression, anxiety, fear etc., the spiritual journey becomes truly focused on the attainment of the highest. It's not where you will worry about the mortgage, what the kids are doing, or whether your hair is falling out, (or losing its color). More importantly it is not where you are going to be angry all the time, because things don't work out the way they should.

You become able to accept what is happening with serenity, without losing your ability to change things, and this is where fearlessness comes in because you're not frightened of outcomes or what people think of you.

You really get the prayer. (Purpose).

"God grant me the serenity to accept the things I cannot change".

Along with the wisdom to change the things you can.

So here is not just a fake wishy-washy think stance. This can be a powerful possibly even seemingly aggressive stance when needed, which is delivered without any internal anger, and is driven by courage.

"And the wisdom to know the difference".

We are based in and around the Divine Reality and not in our illusion driven ignorance.

Tam 2

(Tam is the core "sound" mantra for *Tara*)

See life and try to feel the oneness with all, even though there are specifics of separation such as work, relationship and living situation. There always seems to some degree, to be fear and anxiety about the specifics of life, regarding what will or won't occur.

However, this emotional and thought train is the minds reactivity that is a residue even when we are in deep meditation.

We cannot stop being ourselves no matter how enlightened we become. Even annoying little habits remain, or harmless ones.

We can, however, mentally receive all of this as just mind and body continuum. It's all quite normal for human beings to be at times fearful or anxious for instance. Even at clinical or pathological levels of say depression or anxiety, it is still only a mental health disorder that can be managed reasonably successfully with the right application and the right resources. "Treatment works". It's statistical otherwise we would not have myriads of services often spending taxpayer's money.

By being focused on one's True Self it becomes entirely possible to limit both the presentation and effects of any psychological distress. The same could be true for physical illnesses with as pain. Disease can again be "re-seen or re-formatted".

Just stably being in the "witness state", changes significantly the impact of any disorder or disease. This witness state has been described in Vedanta philosophy as the soul's overview and oversight of all activities in the world of Maya. In Buddhism there is also the meditation process which has been popularized in western culture as a mindfulness way that has therapeutic benefit.

All can be changed, because when we recognize our "Strengths" as opposed to our weaknesses we go about life in a very different way. (See also literature on the "Strengths Model" in mental health care).

So, we are talking about modifying something, (say reactivity), so is only part one of the spiritual process. The other part is recreating or creating anew. Being significantly in touch with the Transcendental Soul we move out to another world of Being.

Otherwise, we are like clothes stuck in a dryer going round and round, and yes getting pretty dry, but not out on the line in the sun. Swishing around in just recovery and hope.

Not a bad thing but nevertheless not the full ticket!

We need to investigate then how we can live *beyond* our fears and anxieties, by remaining in Divine awareness, even in the midst of daily activities.

By going beyond or transcending, we then move into a space of re-creating where we are no longer just recovering or just managing. Various mental health, addictive and psychological issues especially are put on one side while we get on with our true purpose. (*Realistic Realization or Practical Enlightenment*). This includes the chronic tendency towards fear and reactivity which propels us to behaviors where we seek to self-soothe and possibly leads into all the activities when we descend into substance use, including food. Depression at a clinical level seems to go hand –in-hand at this point.

We have created what is before us per individual and we suffer per individual as a result

Of course, happiness and pleasure is there, but sometimes we are just wrapped up in it either the getting of it, or the wanting, or the holding on. Then if there is an exclusion of having a healthy overview, we don't want to know, until perhaps we hit rock bottom. Therefore, there is not much point in talking to those who are not interested in addressing their pain and remain content to seek pleasure only.

Pleasure though, in a spiritual perspective, is no different than pain, and should equally be addressed by the practitioner of a spiritual process or program. This is all filtered down through the self-identifying process leading to realizing the individual self, (the Atman), as being one with the cosmic consciousness, (Brahman).

Additionally, most of us will need some religious or spiritual activities that are more specific and targeted to help with the gross elements of human existence. This is where we have our own set of prayer, chants, mantas, or liturgies.

The path of knowledge, (Gyana), may be too high a road and unrealistic aspiration for some who also need the devotion to a personal God, which is the yoga of devotion, (Bhakti Yoga). Invariably all of us need to engage in some selfless service to others, (Karma Yoga).

Then there is also the "kingly" pathway or Raja Yoga, where mental and physical specific exercises, including meditation and concentration, are engaged in. (To create a deeper state of spiritual awareness or the "trance" like Samadhi).

There is no reason that anyone cannot sit on higher spiritual levels. The choice is there and available when agreed to. However, it will take time for the benefits of any spiritual endeavor to filter down into our daily business and purify the gross elements of our activities. This includes our diet, use of substances or food to self-soothe, and distractions such as media and Internet, used to avoid facing the truth of our existence, with its daily anxiety and fear levels.

There is always the potential for Divine Grace as we seek contact with our Deity or Higher Power. Then our guiding angels, guardian angels, or spirit guides act as aspects of Divinity and move to support us in our endeavors. We may actually see and hear them or feel them. Or more commonly, otherwise realize their connections with us.

Some spiritual practitioners may be intimately connected with their Gods, spirit or forces, whereas others may just have hope that they are out there, or something is out there that will help them in some way.

The true transformation does occur eventually after persistence, and that may include treating the various more overt issues such as significant depression, addictions, and obsessive bad habits. We may also be afflicted with quite severe personality defects such as narcissism, or a tendency to be aggressive and paranoid about everything around us. These "defects of character" all need attention, and that can be done spiritually by prayer etc., but may need more concrete work as well through therapeutic support and counselling. Psychiatric support does help when it's really indicated!

The transformation occurs when the small ego-based self or personality aligns to the Truth which is another zone than our inherent nature. Not just a change or different person. We want to be a different Being which is our own Divinity shining through and lighting up our daily business.

I am!

This comes after we ask: Who am I?

We then are able to do mindfulness, be meditative, and be self-aware. We can be in the moment because we are the moment!

Suffering occurs. Yes that's what we get for being a changeable entity in a changeable world.

But, the world and all its mind or body combinations has a substrate under this illusory Maya. This transitory circus show! This is the unchangeable Soul beyond ego and personality.

When we are hurt enough from the surface business, we go down and dive deeper and deeper, dependent on to how desperate we are. We even become willing to self-surrender to a Higher Power or Deity and give it "handing it over" a "whirl over".

We want that energy. That consciousness.

As we go to God so God comes to us

As we claim our true selves, we receive the Grace that hastens the process.

Life then is not a problem. It then is our teacher, our means of liberation, and a source that we can express gratitude for. No need then to justify either your life and its complexity, or your associated search which sometimes seems to go on in another dimension. A seemingly circular fashion at times, which nevertheless, even if we don't see it, is completely interconnected with our ever-present Divine nature.

The Divine as me is the nicest stance, but this doesn't mean we are special!

It's only if we can see and pay homage to the Divine in the other person.

Is this realistic?

Is this realistic given we tend to be reactive in relationships?

Probably relationships are the number one minefield far as our emotions and serenity management is concerned.

However, the position of seeing the Divine as already manifest is true, because it is what really already exists.

We may seem to be creating a new way of living with a spiritual vision and processes, whereas in fact we are going nowhere in a journey because we are not even on one. (From a higher philosophical perspective of course).

More likely we are choosing to accept the Truth but allow it to have overarching Dominion only to the degree that we let it be so.

And this is not surrender!

We may put out our individuated sense of divine consciousness to request that we get assistance in the work of overcoming the small ego base personality.

Of course we fear letting go, and it is this fear that actually prevents us from letting go.

It seems that the fear is based on this: "oh dear I will have nothing left and I will cease to exist".

However, it's true that some personality will remain, even if you become the new Buddha or a big Guru. Also, humans by nature have a flight or fight automatic response, which means that some degree of fear and reactivity also remain.

It's all in our nature to be fearful, anxious, and reactive. And it's in our nature to retain petty defects, such as picking one's nose in public.

The spiritual pathway or journey is more than about being in recovery, even though that person seeks "healing" from the past.

Of course, we all want perfect cures, with perfect

released from what ails us.

Therefore, the therapeutic or self-help managed interventions will have limitations, which is not to say they won't work very well, especially in terms of recovery or remission.

The true spiritual path goes, however, into the transcendental and seems sees recovery and remission as almost incidental.

This is when we move into a new way of living in a new home for our soul and enter into the Higher Rooms of existence.

This is when we bring the Divine Light into our darkness, or we walk into the light and therefore leave the darkness behind.

Then perhaps, probably, we hope, we leave behind our negative personalities, or rather all the unhelpful mechanisms in our lives, keeping what's essential for physical well-being. This includes keeping those ingrained petty habits that run their own show. (As long as they do no harm).

We no longer label ourselves with dysfunctions we got from our psychiatrists, therapists and spouses. We are not called depressed, alcoholic, borderline, narcissistic or neurotic.

We also move past the need for PTSD, addiction and so forth, simply because we leave the past behind and enter the future of Divine Sanity

Doing this requires a leap. Add on also a choice to make the leap, and to stay with the pathway chosen to Spiritual Nirvana.

Even with this choice, healthy action can be difficult within the turmoil of everyday life which does not want to let go. Even the monks and the nuns get this problem!

That's why we have a Deity, a Higher Powers, Incarnations or even God. (Maybe a Goddess).

They are there to help us to be present, by them being present in our lives

We are then truly in the moment

Some have angels, some get transmissions, some get

channeling

In the pathway enumerated in previous writings there is Kundalini Yoga. In this line of practice we attain the realization. We get Samadhi which is Saguna. "*Sa*" meaning "with", and "*Guna*" meaning the quality or form. Without form is Nirguna, where "*Nir*" means "without". Those who seek the path of knowledge or Gyāna, will seek the Nirguna and those who need or want a personal God stay with the Saguna.

It matters not if the realization is of the Personal Divine or Cosmic Consciousness.

However the transcendent impersonal form realization is historically considered difficult for "ordinary" humans to attain. It seems to be a domain of rigorous reclusive introspection or renunciation, such as obtained by monks, nuns and saffron-robed yogis who meditate all day, based in monasteries and caves.

However now this is the transformation for our age, and it is within.

Therefore, it does not really need the external cave dwelling or robes. Boots, shoes, suits or T-shirts will do!

More importantly it's not about changing the job, the marriage, and the relationships.

Especially the relationships!

Seeking comfort is a distraction from the real work of overcoming fear and reactivity, let alone desire. However, we are in situations where we need to be. This is in any given time, if we can accept, it learn from it, and transcend it.

If we fight the dream, the illusion or impermanence, we support it in some ways. If we bring it into the light of Truth the darkness disappears along with the "crazy dream".

We are free, not only from our need for salvation, but from the journey also.

We are already where we want to go!

Chapter 6
"Statements" or Aphorisms

The Deity or God/Goddess is beyond description, but could be seen as the totality of all and thus is "perfect or complete". This creation and the creator and are then "Whatever": *Life and the Universe.*

This phenomenal world can then be seen as perfect for our requirements whether that is to enjoy, ("eat, drink and be merry"), or to do penance in caves, and return to out Divine state.

Incidentally we are already Divine, but are enveloped in the illusory powers of Maya, and thus think we are body/mind, personality and ego.

We are perfect and complete as we are.

Whatever is produced of the Cosmic Consciousness cannot be a duality of good and evil. Or enjoyment and pain cannot be different! (This is "advanced consciousness")!

The whole is complete in itself. But the universe emanates from Him, (or Her).

Everything must then be in complete balance. Even

when that balance is chaos, pandemics, wars and planet loss.

(As happens apparently at the end of this era called Kali Yuga).

Everything animate or inanimate that is within the universe is controlled and owned by the one Deity.

This is because ones Deity varies. It can be inside of a religion or as a Higher Power or something else.

We all choose something different as per our culture, religion or belief system. We all possible differ even if slightly on an individual basis when it comes to our perception of, say, the Buddha or the Christ. (Even if we are in the same "subset", of Catholicism or Tibetan Buddhism etc.)

One should be happy therefore to accept only those things necessary for life. Of course, we all want for ME.

We have a quota, as our lot in life, because we are sustained by life itself, which is of course Divine. Our delusion within consciousness identifies via our ego/personality with the external worlds and sees our wants and desires as of primary importance.

This then leads to the illusion of not having enough, not being good enough, and in its extremities may lead to self-harm and suicidal thoughts! Matter is impermanent, since it is created in birth and destroyed in death. The external world ages and changes. Your house will be gone in a thousand years! Probably.

This process, including death, or loss, usually gives rise to fear, and we want to "get stuff fast", as we don't understand the real issues nor ask the right questions.

Who am I?

What am I?

What is my real purpose?

The answers: My name. A human. To procreate

But are you just a name? Just a human? Just here to produce offspring?

If you're happy with that, throw this book away!

We usually don't know who we are. Because we don't pursue the questions related to meaning and consciousness. We ignore them, for logical and very human reasons. Too scary!

We want to control nature also.

It's scary because we then have to confront the facts that all is just momentary, and pleasure, drugs, alcohol, sex are not a permanent solution to birth, old age, death and disease.

Surrender seems like loss of all, but acceptance allows for real freedom from fear. You find out who you really are and what the world really is.

The world has been here for a long, long time. Don't worry about it. Worry about your identity and the basic questions of existence: What is reality? What is experience? Who is experiencing? These spiritual questions can take you to a blissful alternative.

Whatever you do will garner learning

Culminating into knowledge, eventually.

Acceptance requires that you lose your ego/personality. Except the useful bits!

There is nothing like a suitable Mantra, to "shortcut" the whole process.

Usually that means guidance, and possibly a living Guru.

We all are a collective and individual consciousness simultaneously. We are all seeking true pleasure.

We all are seeking the ultimate truth. We all are seeking immortality, an end to all misery/nothingness.

Mantra - it is a combination of special sounds and vibrations that purify space, body, mind and consciousness from negative energies. Mantra – it is an ancient sacred formula that gives a powerful Divine energy, and it is the key that opens the way to the Supreme Divine knowledge. Repeat the mantras as much as possible.

A Rosary also helps with concentration on the mantra and meanings, for the beginner.

Again, get advice on this from somewhere (The Internet is better than nothing)! *Hari Om Tat Sat*

Goddess Inspired.......

My Goddess has brought me to an experience of craziness, and then out of it into sanity.

Both I now own.

I am sane and insane all at once!

I professionally help others with mental health issues, whilst myself have in the past received support for my own mental health difficulties. All at once or at the same time.

My Deity tells me to accept all, and not to run or want something better, or want my life goals achieve now. Alternatively, achieve what I want.

In other words, do not be an ego-based personality.

Surrender all, to let the Divine Shakti be what runs life.

Do I do this?

I try.

Sometimes my prayers seem to be answered, but mostly it just takes too long! That is my ego persona and its wants.

However, one thing to me is clear.

I am devoted to whatever is out there that is considered to be the Higher Power, in whatever form.

I know this is my past, present, and future and thus can be more focused on the now, the present moment.

I practice meditation with mantras to energize my kundalini energy through the chakras. I do this for myself, but also seek to radiate out a healing, serene and peaceful force that will work for others through their chakras or energy centres in a healing manner.

It is still a moment-to-moment matter.

Not tomorrow or later.

First, is this per breath focus, and then focus on what is in front being experienced now, mentally, physically, and psychically.

Accept it, let it wash over, enjoy it sometimes, but experience that as being part of the Divine Cosmos.

Feeling that experiencing as one's own Divinity filtering into the human life.

Feel it and live in it

The *Sat, Chit, Ananda.* (Existence, Knowledge, Bliss).

Karma

You choose desire and want.

You act and then get.

You reap the results of action.

It is Karma.

Why though?

Why choose a job, a partner, or even a life to be born into?

Something to do with learning perhaps?

Maybe so that a person's human nature can become spiritual in nature.

Even when it comes to being on the spiritual journey, it seems you want to get it as a human experience.

Not necessarily as a true spiritual experience. Not as a spiritual experience dictated by the higher powers that be, but one on own terms. We continue to hold of our own scheme of how our spiritual future will pan out.

How it is meant to work for *me.*

It is all about *me!*

To know and be known at a higher level requires a jump away from Karma.

Transcend it.

You have may have had some spiritual experiences, brief, momentarily, or more extended because you are a regular practitioner. Apart from these experiences, you may well be based psychically n your everyday. A life that every day comes about dictated by rules. Karma rules. Your intention and focus may however change when you have "had a taste". (Of the Transcendental Divine)

The potential is there to be at one with your true Divine Self, even as you insist that you are who you say you are.

Some people are impacted by experience of mental health issues. Or physical issues. With regard to how it affects their spiritual practice, this experience of ill-health can hold a person back spiritually, if not addressed. On the other hand, sometimes a very powerful spiritual awakening or urge is driven by those very same mental and physical experiences. They can be painful. Anything that holds you back from your journey needs to be addressed, even need to be addressed anyway, to have a decent life. You may well require treatment, medication, therapy, or whatever works for you as an individual. Just to become available to be strong for this spiritual journey.

However, in mental health terms, if you call yourself a depressive or an alcoholic or trauma sufferer, then there is also another danger. Whilst recognition of these disorders is certainly beneficial, there is a risk of being stuck and in a loop, where ones only identity is that of an unwell person. Certainly not a spiritual person. A person may become enmeshed in the mental health system, potentially ending up with getting more and more medication, and experiencing illness that is more chronic, side-effects, and pain. Even more sadness is not what is wanted!

Goddess Inspired

Deciding to go this way definitely brings about its own Karma, and it may not be pretty!

You can decide to go another way.

Surrender to the Divine.

The Karmic outcome is Light.

This does not prejudice the judicious use of medication therapy counselling, or whatever is useful If it gets you to the point of functional stability; all good

Then you can do the real work.

The work that takes you beyond Karma and into the spiritual realms.

You become Divine because you are.

From a Karmic perspective, you can find that the mental and physical issues may well become: "background noise"

They might not go away.

They might not even change much.

People often do not get much cure for a physical serious ailment, just because they pray to God, or do the meditation. Maybe of some benefits practical benefit, as there is scientific evidence for the benefit of meditation and prayer. Both mentally and physically in terms of health.

Perhaps more important is to get the spiritual perspective and alignment with the Divine Energies. For me this is alignment with the Shakti, the Goddess energy, which is the overarching consciousness, playing out into the visible world

Then there is essential healing.

Essential, because is about freedom from identity with the body mind complex.

Sounds too hard!

Impossible?

Has been done. A lot!

If you read spiritual books and read about the journeys of spiritual teachers and gurus, you will find that there are many men and women who have attained very high levels of spiritual enlightenment.

In other writings, I have talked of the power of the sound, and of the healing nature of certain sounds. A transforming power of one's chosen mantra which brings about a profound "alternative" karmic affect. This can be as much as full transcendence of Maya. It can be beneficial regarding physical and mental elements. It can be very practical to do with the attainment of one's desires and needs in the world.

Your mantra is what suits you as a person, and this may be driven by your religious preferences. Ideally, it is something that you have received or learnt about through a good teacher, mentor, or coach. Or, guru.

The Truth about you can be harnessed and manifested through sacred sound and meditation.

You already Divine, because you are part and parcel of a universe that is Divine.

You may continue to follow and choose the collective statements about your being and behave in order to get what you want or think you need. Seek then to achieve by human endeavours.

Spiritual endeavours on the spiritual journey will send you to another Karmic dimension.

Self-realization, Enlightenment, *Nirvana/Moksha.*

What then happens to the world? *Life and the Universe.*

You experience it then differently, because you are lifting yourself and being lifted by Divine Grace up into the light.

You see your fellow human as Divine

You accept all around you, and know you are in learning experiencing, "regulated' by the Divine Presence in all.

You begin to let go of your compulsions, dependencies, and unhealthy struggles. Or, they begin to fade away of the own volition.

Fear and reactivity do not exist in the light

The Divine Grace can reach out to you.

If you reach out!

Aphorisms

We are making our life

We think act and reap

"As ye sow".

Also, unfortunately, regarding mental health, as we think so we attract.

We attract the darkness, the fear, and anxiety, through our own thought processes.

Is it all our fault?

However, all is not lost. The means to self-correct or self-manage is present along with the problem.

We have resilience, usually.

We have personal strengths.

We have functional abilities to cope and manage, usually.

It is a human phenomenon that some will undergo horrendous trials and experiences and come safely out the other end. The same can happen with our depression, addictions, obsessions, and other disturbances of the mind.

Firstly, all experiences seem to occur for a purpose, and that is a learning one.

Hopefully a spiritual one.

The key is to understand that we can challenge and change our thought processes, for a start.

We believe we will suffer terribly if we lose our job, marriage, memory, health, etc.

The thoughts accompanying the beliefs create fear piled upon fear.

The darkness creates more darkness.

The core thoughts that disrupt or energize, are all about an intrinsic energy.

What we are really made of.

(Like the scientists who say we are nothing more than a dense bundle of oscillating atoms),

Say I am only a body/mind and all is lost.

Say I am a Divine spirit and all may be saved.

Choose the Light.

It is not about burying ones head in the sand and ignoring "reality".

It is simply about releasing an identity, a reactivity.

"I am the Witness".

The mind will go on creating scenarios, even though the reality is that is temporary.

We All will die! (Just to get started on this topic).

We react to death and the processes of moving towards it. (Called "Life"). Then we go downwards spiraling sometimes into darkness, mental sickness, stress, and fearful reactivity.

Why?

In conjunction with our God, our Higher Power, or with our Divine self, we can release fear, grief, and reactivity.

It is not present there! (In our "Higher Rooms" or Divine Space we are free).

A simplification perhaps, our True self is full of Light and free to interact without getting bogged down in the ego-based personality processes.

We can still grieve, love, maybe even lust!

However, it is all seen for what it really is, just like waking from a dream. Or, realizing we were frightened in the dark by a snake that turned out to be a length of rope!

Thus, we accept our thoughts and our mental convolutions in reactivity, knowing that they pass of their own accord. The day will pass; your shift at work will pass, as indeed will all the things that you call "mine".

"Fight or flight" is now mostly redundant. We are not cave dwellers and are slowly changing to meet the modern age of technology. Oh yes, I forgot to mention. We are now getting into even more serious trouble, brain wise!

I lived initially with no TV, and no phone in the house.

Forget about the internet. Forget about social media.

We still have our ego-based personality, with its foibles. Modern information technology and artificial intelligence is now adding all whole new range mental health disorders. Of the individual as well a societal. It's progress because we can give new medication, explore the electrical and chemical balance within the brain.

Are we keeping up with the downside? The statistics for mental health issues among the young are scary. The prevalence of self-harm is scary. (Because it seems to be increasing). Technology is progressing exponentially and we will need to meet the challenge of mental health issues. But can we?

The ancient seers and sages had answers. For all time. For any eventuality. They said we can be liberated, have our freedom, be able to step back from confusion and the scary daily news.

Connect with Divine within us or connect to your external Deity if that is your way.

Be the Witness.

This is where some techniques can be handy. My choice: the use of mantras in conjunction with Kundalini Yoga, and the devotional aspect of practice directed towards the Goddess Shakti.

It could be a religious/spiritual smorgasbord or "menu" of your choice. I am not pedantic about what works best. I leave that to the bigots and the fundamentalists!

Fear and anxiety is obvious but the lowering of mood, or the increase of substance use, can creep up unnoticed. Until too late.

This decline can even include "doing good", when this is driven by selfish neediness.

So, take the steps and lift above the darkness, reaching out for your Guides, Gurus, and Deity,

Then as you move towards it, the Divine Grace will move towards you,

Stay focused in G.O.D. –good orderly direction and receive the Divine Grace.

The spirit is here.

All around, throughout, inside, outside, everywhere.

There is a choice to allow the codes of life to say what is right and what is not.

That God is here but being seeing as slightly or possibly very separate.

A Divine being, just part of life.

It's you.

Or, as an external voice.

It will say stop those thoughts

Why?

Because I am here. They go nowhere. They have no function to generate fear reactivity and anxiety.

Why are they there? Good question.

I just **is** and you know it you know it.

Your thought processes may connect positively with bodily advantage into your human experience. You may want this. Most people do the human experience that is. After all that is why we are here. Some karma perhaps. On the other hand, a desire to be in human form. Alternatively, an inheritance decreed by cosmic forces.

It is all very mysterious at times. Any particular religion always wants to give you their specific solutions. Which may help to drive you bonkers!

Remember, you are Divine. I am Divine. All is Divine

Do you want to accept this? What will it mean?

It does not mean anything other than being as you already are. Just in Enlightened. Simple

However, this all probably seems confusing in reality.

Remember therefore, one needs a guide a good teacher, unless you are already there. That means an external living one, if at all possible.

Yes, it will be a human with potentially more foibles and you have.

It is the teaching and guidance that's wanted.

Grab that and even more.

Ignore the rest.

All good

What is your mantra?

Repeat it and the guidance will come whether you have the external guru or not.

If you live life, you remain in life.

If you seek and desire a spiritual life, you move into that world which is more than just human.

Life and the soul's growth are not incompatible.

The external and internal resources required for the spiritual journey are already here.

You make the change by walking the path.

The scenery changes as you move along.

So gradual as to be imperceptible at times.

Yes, you need to know patience is first.

Continued striving is second.

Desire for Divine experience third.

Faith it will all happen is the summary.

Deal with the obstacles. Around them under them over them, through them.

Human habits are not barriers. They can be changed diverted and minimised.

Any human condition is not a big deal.

You can still do what you need to do in the spiritual realm.

Use the teachers like medicine.

Use the practice pathways like transport.

Use the secret words as protection.

The mantra is food for the journey towards enlightenment.

Use all helpful people as your mechanics.

And that's it.

Chapter 7
Spirituality and mental wellness.

While the neuroscientific exploration of religious and spiritual phenomena has advanced, this field of research is still in its early stages. Is there even a huge interest in doing this? Why try to prove something that millions have accepted for thousands of years.

However, the pursuit of scientific "evidence for the existence of God", (for instance), may be useful. (If you care!).

At least for me there is a growing and significant consideration of spirituality, and I also believe this is happening more in the world, even though the daily news says otherwise!

I have been interested in academically exploring the topics I am writing about, including scientific research about spirituality and mental health.

Mantras for mental health

Tap into the Divine power within and without. Use and repeat God's holy Names. Select the mantra of choice, or better still get a mantra from a knowledgeable Guru.
Repeat as much as possible.
From India we have for example the mantras:

> *Hari Om*
> *Soham*
> *Hare Krishna*
> *Rama, Rama.*
> *Om Namah Shivaya*

And many, many more.
Also "seed" mantras associated with the *Chakras* described in my books.

Mentally repeat. (Called *Japa*)
Mantra's power will then do the work for you as desired. (I.e. can be used for wealth or spiritual growth. You choose).
Mantra is vibrational healing, of the soul through to mind, body, and to your environment.

In addition, mantras create a shield of "armour" around you to protect from curses, violence and accidents.
Higher vibration emanating from mantra repetition rises above darkness, or even evil forces.

It is a remedy for depression because you bypass it. It is left behind in the darkness. In the "Higher Rooms" there is only light.

You are not your body and mind. You are the "Witness" Your natural state is *Sat, Chit, Ananda*. Existence, Knowledge, Bliss.
Light is always you as the Divine soul. It is your birth right. You may need to connect with It, even though it is just *there*.

We separate ourselves from Light, we live in darkness. Change perspective and focus
Seek Divine Grace.

The Divine is perfect and complete, and emanations from the Divine, such as this world of *Life and the Universe*, are complete in purpose. Be it your belief in the Goddess as the creature, or God as Him, or as the Big Bang. Whatever is produced in this Cosmic Consciousness is interconnected with sound.

Even though many components emanate, a wide variety of sounds are associated. A sound for each aspect. Thus, there are many mantras and each of the major ones has an extensive history of practice and is seated within a body of ancient knowledge.

Our consciousness identifies with matter, the illusion that is Maya. Matter is created and destroyed at some point of time, but nothing really disappears. Hence, we can agree with much of science here. (The Big Bang is after all a "large sound'). However, we are in fear, and rush around, because we cannot understand the essential essence of both the Transcendent self and the Maya created forms in life. We do not connect with the underlying sound. The mantra makes this connection, and gives us understanding to the point of Enlightenment. After all Maya is just the Goddess going about her business!

We do not ask the real questions. Not what is your name, but what sounds are you composed of?

Our consciousness is ignored. However, we try to control nature. Unless you know yourself as Divine (in sound), all else is just fleeting experience. A trip!

Do not fear, just worry about:

Who am I?

What is reality?

What is experience?

How do I serve?

Find your mantra/s. They will attune you to the collective and the individual consciousness. *Sat Chit Ananda.*

Mantra is a combination of special sounds and vibrations that purify space, body, mind and consciousness from negative energies. Mantra is an ancient sacred formula that gives a powerful Divine energy and is the key that opens the way to the Divine knowledge.

Repeat the mantras as much as possible any number of times.

There is manta science regarding repetition. Use a rosary or *Mala.*

108 times, is considered sacred, as it is the number of Rishis, (holy seers), in the sky, see as stars.

Chant, sing, write, or meditate silently.

The *Mala* is charging with Divine energy and thus is an excellent talisman or amulet. Treat it with due respect!

Kundalini, and mental health.

Kundalini works in the body through the chakra centres. It flows and allows blocks to move. That is physical, psychological, mental, and emotional. Everything.

This can pay out, in the broadest sense. Hopefully, to increase Bliss. Suffering and Bliss. How these words resonate within the religious or spiritual sphere. Kundalini revealed and free to flow is synonymous with a deep spiritual awareness, and a connection with the Divine. However, at some point the full process of energy involvement through the centres or chakras becomes irrelevant. We may do our daily spiritual practice, move into the sphere of knowledge and awareness of a Oneness or around us. So really the whole idea of human Awakening upwards" through the chakras can be dispense with, or reversed, as one becomes more proficient. The same divine energy comes down to enable a somewhat different but still divine experience. From a religious perspective, we worship a divine firstly as external deity, and as a powerful being. We are at risk of being the ostrich. With head buried in the sand; if we are not aligned to divine energy presenting into our human lives, mentally and physically, *as they are*. That is the idea that meditating on kundalini arising may be somewhat misleading.

The purpose and function of kundalini is to enable us to have an experience of the witness stage, where we "sees through" life *as it is*. Ultimately. The kundalini is a holy force aligned to the goddess energy. Otherwise, it may have a connection with the Holy Spirit. It takes us out of our material craziness, but also it takes us through them, not passing by them or burying them. The Awakening does not make us mad or bad, we already were.

We do however have to take what cure we really need to take and leave what we can discard. For instance, much of religion has become distorted over the years, and often serves no purpose or confuses and even destroys us. We need then to see religion as something that can help us only in parts.

Does the concept of depression connected to kundalini and spiritual awakening be seen as a higher process that is trying to connect and balance both of flow and of energy to and from divine consciousness? This meets the needs and aspirations of the human personality.

The kundalini energies may be recognized just as the power of meditation and other spiritual practice is being "discovered". At this point, we can say that psychiatric drugs to some degrees are toxins that may damage the brain, whilst healing the disorders. This is no different from saying that Panadol or aspirin is harmful. Just because we may say that psychiatry is defunct, we can also say the same about religion, or new age, or spiritual practice. In reality if we find a medication that helps us without significant side effects, there should be no conflict between our spiritual practice and scientific evidence-based medicine.

Religion and the Spiritual Journey

Theoretically, the spiritual journey could be made without any references to or involvement with religion, either as belief or practise or as morals. I have not seen and met or read of any spiritual advanced being who was not at some stage intimately involved with religion in some form.

Religion and spiritual practice seem to go hand in hand, although on a closer inspection this relationship is quite tenuous and even hostile. The spiritual seeker may find at a certain stage a burning desire or motivation to escape from or leave behind all or some of previously held beliefs and practices. In some religions, this is ok in others it is high treason.

In some religious cults, any deviance from the accepted moral and social riles a. seen as a fall from grace, a sin, a deviation. Spirituality there is only accepted in the context of the rules. However, it is a fact that no one religion has the control over the world population that its more fanatic adherents would wish for. Some spiritual seekers have and always will hold onto their own faith even of their allegiance to a religion is shattered or becomes insignificant.

The Spiritual Journey is about the goal, the end product notwithstanding the connections made on the way with organised religion, New Age ideas, and scientific therapies. Religion becomes a block to spiritual growth when it interferes with or is allowed to block further evolvement. The concept of God, Deities, Messiahs and Avatars (incarnations) belongs to the realm of the practitioner not to the world of the Realiser, who has become Awakened, Enlightened or Divinely fulfilled. That goal is really quite anarchic, disinhibited, and even destructive in terms of what passes as conventional ways of equating an ordinary life with the Higher Power. Most materialistic everyday strivings seem to be geared to trying to get on with or outwit God in order to achieve ends. God then becomes someone or something "up there and the church or temple becomes a convenient place to off load the guilt or shame generated whilst trying to fulfil basically selfish needs and wishes.

Spirituality does not require a God "up there" nor an edifice to worship in to prove one's goodness to others. The spiritual seeker then, a concerned with how to achieve the goal of Truth. How to begin the journey, (avoiding the obstacles and dead ends). How to find a good path and how to keep on it (avoiding the distractions consolations that divert). In that light all responsibilities are scrutinised, including the value of the religious devotional paths. This examining then becomes a form of yoga, a meditation, and philosophical enquiry.

Devotion which derives from or is associated with the East (Hindu, Buddhism and others), can be freely contrasted with the Western scientific civilisation, which also the tradition of Christian and Jewish monotheism. More recent advent of the "psychological" forms of treatment and the therapies, which have evolved with the fields of mental health, also now propose themselves a solution to life itself in a broader outreach. Many of the New Age practises and the therapy modes seem to be amalgamating and synthesising a total radical approach to the concept of wellbeing and "awareness". (Is this being "Woke")? This would seem to be their good reason for a wide appeal to different body of people with completely new outlook on what is "spiritual searching.

Unless you can get a religion that is non-judgemental. One that accepts a variety of beliefs is worlds away from fundamentalism. On the other hand, just go to the Truth of the matter. What did the Buddha say? What did Jesus say? Not what the patriarchal priests of a man-made religious system would demand us to believe or be dammed eternally!

Another way in is to be Multi Faith. Make of it what works. Seek the Truth and discard the rubbish. Follow the Guru, but not if he/she is into some form of depravity.

Do not tithe! God is Free!

Most regular religion makes depression and mental illness only worse. Often, they are very anti-medication which is also not Truth. Medication, CBT, etc. can be very useful-to a point. But don't get sucked into the mental health system either! Therapists and psychiatrists are not God!

If you are depressed, you often feel lost and without hope. Hence the lure of drugs and alcohol!

You certainly do not want to hear about eternal damnation.

You always were Divine, how would you not be whole? If you have experienced separation, you can return to your Divine Centre and actually know what the contrast feels like.

Separation and suffering is Maya. Illusory-whatever!

(Not real in the first place, or ever. It feels real, until you wake up, from illusion. The Dream!)

Do it while you are still alive. This is what your Deity wants. (Get on your spiritual pathway).

Goddess Inspired

Heaven on earth. The here and now. *Moksha, Nirvana,* is what I write about:

Realistic Realisation and Practical Enlightenment.

Be sane in this place: *Life and the Universe.*

In our human lives we maybe spiritual or religious and are going to pray a lot to God.

I tended to pray from an "I want" perspective. This made it harder for good changes to happen in my life.

I always tended to think that I could make it happen, or what I do created the changes.

What I know is that it does not work this way!

It works better if I let go. It works better if I make the big surrender. Let go of being an ego-based personality, even if it means giving up-called normality.

It is not about quantity it is about quality!

True spirituality then is a radical move towards the transcendental, whilst yet being still in human state.

About being in one's own Divinity yet finding that through external help through Divine Grace. That is because it is very hard to make the change required and is not easily done under one's own human power. It is a bit like asking a drunk to walk in a straight line. When you are affected by intoxication you cannot just do stuff!

No matter how intellectually spiritually astute one becomes, if you remain in a headspace, you ultimately go nowhere, because another spiritual dimension cannot be made by the brains electro chemical processes. (Despite what some research says). Researchers cannot be trusted with God! This is why we need external interventions. We need to give up and give it over to our Deity.

Then we enter a place powered by something else. It seems like our God taking over, but it is simply a natural native Divinity that has been uncovered and allowed to be in-charge.

When that becomes possible, nothing is off the table. That is a spiritual reaction for moment-to-moment life practice, which says, "Yes I am real in this life, but I am real as a spiritual being".

I am experiencing all within and without, like an *app* connected to the eternal Divine Consciousness.

The deeper I go, the more it becomes an easier pathway, with less being frustrated about what's going on in my "real' life.

Transcend

To transcend means to wipe out any negative effect that depression etc. had in your life. But not only that. It is to see the bigger picture and to realize that depression etc. was necessary and to be grateful for it. It is very hard to believe that something as bad is depression can ever be necessary. However, mental health issues may be nothing more than a "slight disconnected". Not from God, as that is not possible. Unfortunately, in serious illness suicide may occur, but then what happens? In re-incarnation terms, you keep coming back to where you stopped learning. It goes on until you keep learning and get the message. In the Cosmic scheme of things, it is a "disconnection". It is being in a state of some seeming separation but maybe feeling being completely cut off from your Source. In spirituality terms, that is an illusion, but it feels real nonetheless. Why do I say this is necessary, as a learning task? Perhaps that state of separation from your Source gives contrasts.

If you always were whole, how would you know what it feels like to be whole? There is no contrast for you to experience wholeness from. However, once you have experienced complete separation you can return to wholeness and actually know what it feels like. As far as I am concerned, this is the point of creation and spirituality. Separation and suffering can never be a permanent state, because it is not real in the first place. It feels very real, but that is only because someone is still caught up in illusion. Imagine life is a dream, and when you die, (or get Enlightened), you wake up.

You return to wholeness and see that the material world is nothing more than a dream. Nevertheless, you do not have to die to realize this Truth. You can realize it while you are still alive. I believe this is what God wants. Heaven is not some far off place in the sky where you go when you were good. Heaven can be experienced here on earth, in the present moment. This is also what is referred to as nirvana or enlightenment. This is the only light in which I can make peace with what happened in my past. Therefore, whether it is true or not is in a sense irrelevant. It is the only explanation that makes sense to me.

Spirituality what is it?

Maybe this is the wrong question.

Maybe it is about why.

Maybe it is about what we are.

We are spiritual beings because we are spirit.

We do not then really have to be spiritual or do spirituality. We are already that.

There is of course choice. Do not believe anything. Chose an external God. Have a religion. Or Lean on science.

Choice or not, what is true is true. The universe and all its elements including there being a deity or not, cannot be other than what it really is.

Ego based personalities would have it otherwise, and hence choices from that direction tend to lean towards the destructive.

Proof.

The history of mankind.

The incidence of suffering overtime and today it is horrible.

There is also too much mental health disorder, and we are seeing what seems to be an ever-increasing trend towards high levels of depression and anxiety. This of course comes with high levels of suicide.

I defy you to say that there is a lot of sanity about, in our world.

So, I go with what is Truth.

Because it does set me free.

It means that I am free.

Free from the lower ego-based activities of the human mind body complex and this earth universe complex.

I can be in the body mind, but I am a witness of its activities.

When I choose this, I move into another level of vibration, of spiritual being. I am a spiritual being having a human experience.

The auras around us. The planes of existence around us, the realm of the extended Cosmos, all caught us in our dream. This dream that we are "so on so such a person or have so many children, and work at such and such a company.

We then suffer due to just being ourselves. We are then subject to fear anxiety sadness and reactivity.

We get into dependencies on substances or behaviours and may experience clinical levels of mental health disturbance.

Often it is not our fault it seems. We experience abuse, trauma, unhealthy or poisonous environments, poverty, bullying. We get PTSD or some elements of effects from our past experience. Now of course we add in the factors of social media and the expectations of society. All this drives us to what?

Possibly drive us to drink. Or whatever our poison is. We take poison to alleviate the poison in our system. We can of course become even crazier.

The reckoning of all this perhaps is to hit rock bottom. Alternatively, perhaps end up under a mental health service or on serious levels of medication.

We may not be able to change much. When we are in severe strife, even though we might try. We may have around us supports in the guise of professional health workers, therapists, social welfare and other options.

The change that occurs when we clean up our act by claiming our birth right.

What does that mean?

I am a Divine entity because I am part of a Divine world created with our enlightenment in mind.

We are here for a purpose, and the ultimate purpose is to return not just theoretically, but realistically do our true nature.

Realistic realisation otherwise known as Nirvana, divine enlightenment, or self-knowledge.

You have to have this in order to be free from fear, but it does mean moving into another level of being. That level is still your native natural spiritual level. It is not something alien or unattainable.

Then *Life and the Universe* becomes something that you see as like a dream. You do not believe it's entirely real even know you're in it and behaving as if it was.

Cannot be real because it changes so much and it is so temporary, and so full of terrifying diseases and disasters. That is before we even get to man's natural stupidity.

You wake up from the dream.

You choose to wake up!

You do then what is needed to find your way. To find your pathway to the truth, your own divine being.

Sounds crazy because if we are divine, we will be on a journey to find out ourselves as being divine.

Yes, it is crazy, and that is how it is.

We cannot get there through our ego personality driven aspirations or actions.

It requires a degree of transcendence or divine grace or guidance of the one who knows already. Who is already enlightened. Who is also practically enlightened, meaning that they can translate what they have into what you need, and they are putting their knowledge of truth into practice in their lives.

If they are just running some sort of cult, all it means is that their ego based personality is on a higher trip. They have turbocharged their nonsense and called it heightened spirituality.

However do not let the trials and tribulations and the obstacles on the way, nor the pits full of snakes and prongs, put you off. Just avoid all that stuff and get don't get side tracked or entrapped in some sort of fundamentalist space - which is another version of the dream - Maya

If your problem is drinking, get the treatment perhaps if it's bad.

If you have, significant depression try some antidepressants and some counselling.

If it is relationship problems, get a good counsellor also.

None of that needs to prevent you or distract you from your spiritual path.

Overall *that* stuff is Plan B.

    I am.

Then I watch. I am the witness.

Then you do the real work.

The work of Truth finding.

You are committed to your spiritual journey. Yes, it's a journey even if you're looking for your own nature.

In the philosophy of the Vedanta there is a mantra

    Soham

    "*I God am*".

However, the truth in that mantra has been historically chanted by only those who were permitted by their culture to practice at that level. Usually monks, the celibate, who live simply on vegetarian food, and certainly did not do "sex 'n drugs 'n rock 'n roll.

You cannot just say I am God, I am the Divine Being, even if it's your true nature.

Why?

Because it might be your ego bound lower self-personality saying this, which will then lead you into even greater strife and trouble.

Therefore, you can believe it and say it and practice it, when you are ready and willing to surrender your life to the Divine Grace, your higher power or your deity - your God.

You have to be willing and ready and actively transcending your ego.

This getting to the point of surrender is I itself potentially a long-lasting journey.

A journey just to qualify for the real journey!

Sounds scary, but that is how it is.

If you are serious, you will do what it takes, whatever that is.

So I suggest, you will need some sandals, staff, and a packed lunch.

Okay. You will need something more that gets you on your way and helps you to continue on your way.

By all means try religion, pilgrimages, prayer, and meditation. Find a teacher, a Guru, mentor, Pastor, or your local holy man/woman.

Read the holy books.

Try to curb your worst excesses

All the above is good, but you cannot get very far without leaving behind a lot of your negative and destructive tendencies.

You can let others tell you who you truly are.

You can let others decide for you what to believe and then how to do what you need to do.

You cannot trust yourself if you have relapsed a few times.

However, you have to do this for you, as your decision as what and how you want to do it. It's your choice to take up the spiritual journey, and your chosen deity will meet you partway part way or even halfway.

Then the Divine Grace will kick in.

So do not rely on others to help you enough, or to tell you enough or to make it easy enough.

And if those you meet on your pathway are too pushy, remember its bigotry and fundamentalism. It is just another diversion.

You are worth nothing less than the Divine as you, and nothing less than becoming Divine down to the toes of your feet, into your real everyday life experience.

Return to the Light

There may be a feeling of disconnection. Life can feel meaninglessness, and there can be overarching wish that "I was not alive". A feeling of inner emptiness, (of pleasure), being filled with only fear and reactivity to life around.

There is a concept of the "sick soul", or for alcoholics, it is a "spiritual disease of the soul", as per 12-step programs. There are many people who feel naturally connected with the world, and they have, or are born with an inner resilience, which is well balanced from the outset. This speaks to the findings about inherited disorders including "addictive personalities". If one is not impulsive, and is steady on course to one's chosen career, relationships etc. then unnecessary trouble is kept at bay. On the other hand, those who are experiencing inner conflicts and/or strife in their environment will lack peace and serenity. The stage is set for mental disorders of depression/anxiety and obsessive behaviors. The original word was melancholia, as including the sense of incapacity for joyous experience. This is now one of two parts for the diagnosis of depression, Anhedonia is the loss of enjoyment for what was previously enjoyable. Alongside is the second major symptom, the low mood perhaps experienced as active anguish with a sort of psychical "deadness" not present in healthy life. Loathing, irritation and reactivity combined with fear, do not make for a happy life!

Depression is a dark experience. A black dog or black hole. Shame and blame then attaches itself, especially if there are episodes of substance abuse. Life can become a crisis.

So what is this disharmony of the individual soul and self, and the world? Why have dark emotions and crazy impulses, and why aren't we full of positive, harmonious, and peaceful emotions?

What wrong with God's creation would say those who are skeptical about a kind and loving Creator!

My disconnection propelled me into becoming a monk in India at age eighteen. Then into a career in mental health.

Some claim something "other" holds them back from deaths door and offers hope.

The complex interweaving of soul and Cosmic Soul, lead to my *Practical Enlightenment*. Not just a spiritual trip, but also a space where I can realistically serve others in my *Realistic Realization* space.

Yes, my sense of healing is Goddess derived for She is my Deity. I have no difficulties with other beliefs as I am Multi Faith.

Meaning can exist in the depth of the dark places. The sick soul can find the healing light and receive the Divine Grace.

A long and painful process can be bypassed with the help of Guides and Gurus. It can be done in this life!

I saw the possibility of happiness, but it is not the ordinary happiness. It is Ananda, the Bliss of Consciousness. Along with spiritual consciousness as Chit, and spiritual Truth as Sat.

Sat, Chit, Ananda. The end product or desired result from the study and practice of Vedanta.

Happiness is something vastly complex, and includes the "dark forces", because it subjugates then, not eliminates them.

Evil or Satan cannot be separate from the Divine Oneness, otherwise there would not be a monotheistic God, only Duality. This is an issue or problem that Buddhism and Hinduism don't have. (Even if they seem to have multiple gods). "Idol worship", does not necessarily mean that the worshiper is Dualistic in faith. It's the fundamentalists that seek to criticize other beliefs!

Natural evil is not a stumbling block when it is swallowed up in the Deity of one's choice.

Healing and harmony can take place not by denying or ignoring, but by treating professionally when indicated, whilst working to undermine the causative darkness and find a pathway that ensures a return to the Light. It is still what one essentially is, a Divine Being yoked with the Cosmic Consciousness.

In my long experience, the mental health profession and service default setting has been that we have very little to do with religion and spirituality. Religious beliefs and even spirituality can even be regarded as "odd or strange', and the professional are "suspicious".

After I left India and stopped being a monk, I was embarrassed to talk about my role and practice, once I had started out as a psychiatric nurse. Almost I thought that I had a pathological issue, and psychiatry did not seem to debunk this. Even maybe my religious practices were considered as a symptom of mental illness. (I probably had a few issues and this made it worse). Was I neurotic? As per the Diagnostical and Statistical psychiatry manual was my experience, (religious and spiritual), proof of a psychopathology.

Recent research however is turning things around. Many patients, who have a religion and spirituality, are being seen as people with "strengths', not weaknesses (Look up "Strengths" model). We have resources that help us to cope with life, including, for me, depression and dependency behaviours.

There is now to be considered, normal religious and spiritual experiences, versus religious and spiritual problems leading to mental disturbances. Leading to this is through a strange anomaly, is it may still propose the spiritual is a causative factor. Well God is a causative factor, so I suppose we can blame Him or Her!

Spiritual history as part of my mental health "make-up". Maybe for many. For some it is something so far not considered. It is still there though, certainly if we believe in a Creator.

Do we commonly make use of religion and spirituality in the therapeutic situation? No!

Spirituality involves belief and often surrender to a Higher Power, or similar. God, who is omniscient, is connected integrally with religion, but not necessarily with spirituality.

Our destiny is involved, what is held to be the purpose of their life. My life has been a search for the meaning of *Life and the Universe*, a connection to the Cosmic Consciousness, and in my case, to the Goddess Shakti.

Whilst universal in nature, obviously my views of spirituality are very personal and unique to me and to followers of Vedanta and Tantra. It may be a sacred realm, but in Tantra the profane is *included.* Nevertheless, I seek to promote and find the Light, which includes love, honesty, serenity and freedom from reactivity.

Religion has different beliefs, doctrines. In addition, liturgy, or worship. Spirituality is present throughout and beyond religion.

If religion is fundamentalist and proposes bigotry, it is lost and is an institution of oppression. Divisive, as in leading to war. (Google: War and religions).

History tells us that this had happened from a lot. A lot of blood has been shed in the name of religion. Now we have Isis and Al Qaeda based terrorism of modern time. Religion helps me to practice spirituality, and thus I am Multi Faith. I take what I need and throw away the rest!

Mental health is not absence of mental illness as we all struggle in differing degrees. We are all a bit crazy. Being well-adjusted sounds good, but there are plenty of high functioning alcoholics. In spirituality it's more about responsibility for one's actions, acceptance of uncertainty, courage to take risks.

    The Serenity payer says:

Serenity to accept the things, which we cannot change, courage to change the things which we can change, and the wisdom to know the difference.

I have read that religious well-being refers to the quality of a person's relationship with a higher power; existential well-being, which refers to a person's sense of meaning and their purpose in life. Also, that those with higher levels of religious well-being were more likely to have had depression than those with lower levels of religious well-being!

There are other components to consider, and for me that is when I write about being Divine. You, me, "everyman and their dog". That is when I write about Vedanta, kundalini, and mantras.

Yes, some years ago I could have gotten a psychiatric diagnosis for these proclamations. Alternatively, going back further could be facing burning at the stake for being heretic!

Disorders and Truth.

Although now we see religion and spirituality as part of a mental health clinician's initial evaluation, assessment or questionnaires, it seems sometimes that it has been thrown in because of some pressure. There can be pressure from segments of the "industry" that defer to culture, political correctness, religious groups and more. Then, these issues may not get revisited at various times during treatment, once the initial forms have been filled out.

Some might point to association of spiritual values with psychiatric disorders compared to worship frequency, as per some researchers. However, why go this route. Quite often, a religious or spiritual person who develops say Mania or a Psychosis will be seemingly obsessed about their interests to a dangerous point. Then remember that whatever is normal for a person will come across as abnormal. It all skewed through a severe disorder. I have met patients who believe and talk (incessantly), that they are Jesus or the Virgin May.

So, if the researchers suggest otherwise, so what? They are just researchers, and I believe science can "prove" anything it likes. Religion does the same. It can "prove the Bible is true". Etc., etc.!

Mental illness is allied with often chronic physical illnesses. They can cause people to search for meaning and look outside to God or Higher Power. Even though they may not be involved in religious behaviors group and may say at the same time that they do not really believe in God.

Best not to over interpret anything. Scientific data or possible clinical implications, or what I am writing in my view!

Also, as a Multi Faith practitioner, I reserve my choice to change my mind any time about what I believe, regarding holy books, guru teachings, and even current trends!

My faith in my spiritual devotion to my Deity is my most valued possession.

I cannot say never ever give up, because that is what happens in depression. Asking for help and then finding the right and effective help is necessary.

Remember what Truth is. One's heart knows it. If you don't know – seek. There are guides, gurus and angels. If you pray for them to appear-they will.

The darkness will pass when the light comes back.

I have found a new understanding of God. For me it is the Goddess and my mantras. Mental health struggle have pushed me along- so that is good!

Buddhist meditation helps and mindfulness seems embedded in this way. Science approves!

In my long experience, the mental health default setting has been that we have nothing to do with religion and spirituality. Religious beliefs and even spirituality can even be regarded as "odd or strange', and the professional are "suspicious".

Suicide

Depression is common today, and most get some experience of it in a lifetime. Some are not able to overcome it and remain in a negative state of mind and probably will seek medical or psychiatric help. Depression can lead to suicide, and the thinking behind that may seem "logical" to the sufferer. It also may seem to be an escape from life.

Religion generally strongly condemns suicide. It all very well to say that nothing is solved by suicide. When the soul is to depart from the body, the dying person sees, actions done during the lifetime. (According to many teachers).
What is mostly being focussed on, engages the soul in that state of consciousness.
Hence, why at the time of death chant the name of God. Repeat the mantra!

Attachment will remain in the soul memory and affect future passage onwards. Especially if it predominant in thought at the time of death. Intoxication may have a negative regressive effect on entering the next realm. Unfortunately, so may the morphine given often to relieve pain around that time, because of cancer etc. However, the power of mantra and faith will cut that delay short and re-enable the onward journey.

"I you lead a pious and virtuous life, you will go to heaven" Prove it!
Tibetan Buddhist say that your last thoughts determine the next birth. This is what the sages say, but Christian's mat say, "there is no next birth". What am I to believe?

It up to your choice how you decide to interpret the phenomenon of death.
I hope that that choice turn out to be correct!

I believe the last dominant thought is very important, but that though is very dependent on our spiritual practice, called *Sadhana* in Sanskrit. Even so, some scriptures say that a very bad person can invoke *Krishna or Rama* at the point of death and the emissaries of *Yama Raj,* (King of Death), will be told to go away. This is why I do not pay much attention to the "holy books". There is a lot of twaddle involved in all religions. I am Multi faith, but I take only what I need for my sanity, what makes sense, and occasionally what seems somewhat "provable", by science or evidence. I include here the writings of those who have been realized as more important as they have had the experience and can better advise accordingly.

The bottom line is that at the time of suicide, the thoughts are very dark and negative, and depression is in control. Hence, why some people are placed under the Mental Health Act after serious suicide attempts.

The works of the Yogis clearly state that if the soul departs with thoughts of anger, fear, or hatred for life, then that mental turmoil will be carried on into the next experience. Yogis or Rinpoche's from Tibet have written volumes about the realms of experience, *after death.*

This soul state will determine which realm we go to next. *"It's Karma Man"*.

Suicide then does not solve anything but makes things worse. Hence the value of "suicide prevention" services.

Another injunction is that the soul can become a ghost, for a long time. Perhaps so that the soul can contemplate to the mistake of suicide. Accountability for others response of suffering caused by the person leaving so abruptly may complicate matters, and even attract retribution, such as a curse.

God as creator has an injunction about many behaviours, which seems to vary as per religious beliefs. It pretty clear though on the Divine injunction against suicide. Or is it?
In Japan people have committed hara-kiri, often by self-disembowelling, and there has been societal approval regarding this if deeply shaming act have been committed. I can comment on this area only in regard to the practice of fasting to death deliberately

as a spiritual penance. It has been practice in Eastern religions.

The ancient and tiny faith of Jainism in India, has a tradition called s*anthara,* (literally thinning out), but India's Supreme Court is considering whether to ban the practice as a form of suicide, which is punishable under law.

Some Jains consider that not eating is a nonviolent way to detach from this life and prepare for the next while purifying the soul.

Apparently, a Jain holy man has assisted some 60 other holy men in carrying out santhara. It is performed only when death is imminent, but it's estimated that some 200 Jains fast to death each year, many of them monks.

Blessing or Divine Grace?
Are adversities, calamities, pandemics, dictatorship and communism blessings. Some people love, (some of), them because they strengthen the purpose of life.

Spiritually they turn the mind towards God. ("There are no atheists in foxholes").

How else would we get discrimination and be force us to perform beyond endurance.
What is after all "resilience", (which is the number one preventer of mental health degradation)? "What doesn't kill you makes you stronger".

How do you react under adversity or hardship? We often test ourselves in the work we choose deliberately!
However, why do we not accept eternal bliss and peace? We pray for it, we want it, but do we really accept it.

Even the religious want to purified the body/mind; make themselves worthy for something that is our birth right any way. The Yogis call it *Tapas*. Fast, sit in the hot sun; stand on one leg for months: the list is endless.
It seems somewhat connected with self-harming, especially interesting considering the dramatic rise in self-cutting amongst young women.

Is it some process of purification and strengthening that is realistic or has true meaning. On the other hand, is it an internal spiritual urge for sanity that has become seriously skewed? What is going on, and is there any hint of "blessing in disguise" or even the soul search for meaning?

On the surface-nothing!

However, there is some idea that we cannot proceed in life without one confronting adverse conditions and circumstances. Through it seems experiencing pain, adversity and loss. This may include self-harming. The wise person will allow the effects of the past, even if traumatic, to be "suffered" in patience, serenity and faith, without seeking to interfere by one's own ego personality driven actions.

Hence the need to surrender to ones Higher Power, and seek the Divine Grace.

Om Tat Sat   Om Tat Sat   Om Tat Sat

Chapter 8

Spirituality in *Life and the Universe*

I thought I would have to write a book if I was to describe my spiritual practice, experience and journey to date. However, my practice to date has become changeable firstly due to rec-connection with the philosophy I held in India enhanced though some new perspectives.

I have agreed to do my practice to my best of my ability:

I am willing to release the idea of who I am or what I have been to receive the new.

I am willing to release the attachments I have had, or may still have, to what I think I am or should be.

I accept myself as worthy of this passage.

Depression, Addiction, and Spirituality

Spiritual people may struggle with different types of addiction.

They may experience depression. (Some more severe than others). One of the most interesting aspects is the recognition that prior or within the depression, most of them were rather disciplined, in control of things and life events, and even "succeeding". This is also a reminder to me that before and during my own experience, I was often optimistic with a strong sense of accomplishment. I believed in my ability to achieve, but when experiencing significant depression, it was very difficult to keep this sense within me.

Is it possible that the initial cause of depression in the first place has to do with a very high expectation for oneself? The expectations that may be imposed externally about being spiritually "good" or being "perfect in God's presence". Spirituality seems to be about finding the essential self within - the presence of God. The only way to come to God though seems to be to come the way we essentially are. If we are anything else, we will only end up dishonoring God.

Spirituality is God's invitation to us in all aspects of who we are. Spirituality is that space that allows us to just be and be ok with who we are. It negates any attempt to be what society wants us to be. It negates any attempt to find the high in spiritual experience. It "is what it is." It is not going out looking for God and proving yourself to God. It is in knowing that God is in the very *"isness"* of us.

This leads to a question. Is it possible that certain understandings of spirituality can lead to depression and/or addiction and not the other way around? Personally, while I see that it is possible that pondering spiritual ideas can lead to depression, it is equally possible that the opposite is true. "Depression experience" can also be a central part of the spiritual path. Some say we must go through a Dark Night of the Soul to attain spiritual growth, and that it is wrong to see depression as somehow negating our spiritual growth. "Happy times" are not necessarily the most growth producing.

I led a very disciplined life as a monk in my twenties but have since found that depression caused more changes in my actual behavior than disciplined spiritual practice ever did. It seems that what we become as a result of facing the dark times is thetransformation. Perhaps "normal" people can go about their lives pretending everything is fine; we cannot. We are faced with conditions or disorders that grab our attention and will kill us if we do not take action and turn it into our advantage. Seeing the advantage can give you the insight to use every tool at your disposal to turn your "curse" to benefit.

Spirituality is a topic of increasing interest to clinicians, but there is a diversity and lack of clarity of understanding. Conceptual components of spirituality include "relatedness, transcendence, meaning/purpose, wholeness, and consciousness". This is in opposition to "moroseness, uselessness, lack of energy, inability to sleep, and a poor attitude toward life in general", (among other symptoms of depression).

According to recent statistics, depression, is practically an epidemic, with over 70 million people suffering from its effects, Thus, we want more spirituality and less depression. More happiness, ingenuity, energy, and ability to reach a higher potential in life.

Some very talented people struggle with different types of depression and/or addiction. Some committed churchgoers or practitioners of other religions and monks or priests struggle also. Generally, it is hard to tell whether depression comes first or the addictive/obsessional behaviours. So sometimes a person who is very capable, organised and has a strong sense of morality may succumb to addiction as well as depression. There is a view that oversensitive persons who seek perfection in many areas may be easily subject to negative moods, when they believe they have not performed or achieved whatever it is they are supposed to.

It can be worse for someone who believes that they have found some source of mystical belief and has had an experience of God or a Higher Power. Then addiction and depression can feel like or seem like a fall from grace, an idea or belief itself, which can compound the problem. In another perspective, we could say that addictions or depression may drive the search for truth and sanity, and lead to spiritual practice or religious participation. Some religions say that we will become perfected beings, (eventually!). Whoever is writing or whatever the Scripture, there seems to be an exhortation to hold onto faith, as that will lead us onwards and upwards and out of our messes. Whether that is true or not is something else! Faith may just be a support to hang onto, and spirituality may be a hope giver and purpose or context provider.

There is an issue about the difference between religion and spirituality, and whether one or the other is more likely to help cure, or from another opposite perspective, to cause problems.

In depression, there is poverty of mood and the lure of something which gives a mood burst is very tempting. Nobody wants to feel dead even if in the depression one can want to be that. The addict gets momentarily times of feeling not just alive but super alive, only to plunge down in the comedown. In addictions at some point there can be moments when one feels the presence of a higher reality, and then there is some hope because when this is truly felt there is an immediate sense of relief albeit temporarily. It may be then that dark sadness heralds a drive to find meaning to go past the sense of loss of pleasure, disenchantment and avoidance of activities of life.

Even for a health professionals the whole area of spirituality and religion may seem to be a somewhat empty vista, even a foreboding or forbidden territory. We have to wonder why this is and what it is that affects even health professionals and may even give cause us to skirt around this territory. One can come up with a lot of reasons of course. Look at the history of religion and the pain it caused. Look at spirituality focused practices and see how fundamentalist some people have become even without a mainstream religion. Therefore, the search for meaning in life could be associated with a higher degree of malady. The keyword here though is - associated. It seems one has to find one's own meaning in this paradox.

There sometimes seems to be no reason to be here apart from getting brief periods of pleasure artificially. Therefore, having a purpose and reason to be here is a protective factor, and it may help considerably in prevention of self-harm and suicide. Religious and spiritual treatises tell us that we will achieve afterlife as a result of healthy activities, and that deliberate termination of life may cause problems with these processes. As a result of suicide, we might not go to heaven. On the other hand, if we believe in future lifetimes and rebirth, we may have to come back to start the whole process over again and re-experience our problems. There is also the issue of what we are thinking about at the time of death. If this is dark black material thought processes, we may find ourselves in a dark black space.

Why do people on their deathbed suddenly feel the fear of God, suddenly see the light, and get the blessings? The spiritual teachers exhort us to turn to our Lord, our Divinity, and take up some meditation practice or worship and pray. The power of the Divine Name is much vaunted as is self-surrender and faith that your guide will always present you with the requisite guidance.

Problems themselves in life do sometimes seem to have a purpose. If we live long enough to look back over lengthy periods, we may say, "well that caused me a lot of pain and I've learnt so much more. I became so much stronger and more capable". There is always a test when going through difficulties, sufferings or just daily business. There does however seem to be a purpose, just as in going to school as a child gets more ready for life and learns perspective as well as knowledge. All the other growing up things that we experience make us into a "well adjusted" adult. One hopes!

Spirituality: scientific v personal perspectives.

While the neuroscientific exploration of religious and spiritual phenomena has advanced, this field of research is still in its early stages. Is there even a huge interest in doing this? Why try to prove something that millions have accepted for thousands of years.

However, the pursuit of scientific "evidence for the existence of God", (for instance), may be beneficial both for science and religion.
The human experience of religion is there, and the impetus of the spiritual minded to explain the experience has been there since the whole issue started. Humans do want to know how spiritual and religious practice affect the mind, brain, body, and behavior. Scientific research may shed new light on the complex workings of the human brain as well as the relationship between brain states and body physiology. This may contribute to theological and philosophical perspectives.

Measures of autonomic nervous system activity seem to be the popular way to approach specific practices such as meditation or prayer. There are positive data outcomes for the benefits in areas such as blood pressure and heart rate. There are other measurements that can be applied to different religious-based practices.

For me the most important measures of spiritual phenomena are subjective. I can try to describe it in terms of various cognitive, behavior, and emotional parameters. Furthermore, I try to define my experience as "spiritual" distinguished from my "normal" experience or as different from what I know about other approaches. (Such as atheism).
I know something is happening, but it is not immediately observable to me, more in the nature of subtle ongoing "improvements", (which is really waffle!). In addition, I get a range of experiences from "nothing's happening" to "did I really experience that". I know I have experienced what others could diagnose as significant depression. However, at the time I was not always aware of my misery. It just was.

At least for me there is a growing and significant consideration of spirituality, and I also believe this is happening more in the world, even though the daily news says otherwise! I have been interested in academically exploring the topics I am writing about, including scientific research about spirituality and mental health.

There seems to be a broad consensus that spirituality is an important dimension of human experience, particularly in the settings of illness and adversity, and is typically associated in a beneficial way with measures of health status, coping, and well-being. There also seems to be a substantial level of interest on the part of health professionals, although in practice I am not seeing it in my daily business.

I try to incorporate spirituality into care-giving or professional work in the mental health field. I am also wary of this approach! (Even though in my readings on the topic, spirituality was viewed as a broad aspect of human experience, having to do with meaning and purpose of life). It does motivate and inspire me to "keep on keeping on" at the least, and to do much, much, more, (at times).

It is definitely not always easy to talk about my life in the context of how spiritual experiences are a part of it, but as far as my work goes, it helps me to honour the Divinity in others and not judge them. It helps to also learn from them and see in them their strengths. (See *Strengths Model* used in mental health practice). For me Spirituality is clearly about seeing people as unique human beings that are Divine parts of the Divine Consciousness. Cultivating my own spirituality makes a difference in how I not only see people, but also how I deal with frustrating when working with some clients and situations. I can have strength, and remain at peace, even when things are not looking so good. I feel I can "heal" better and more.

Apart from gaining a sense of meaning, and personal satisfaction, I can believe I am an instrument of my Goddess. Incorporating spirituality in my care of others requires that I respect their Deity, their male God or formless Consciousness. I can only be facilitator of their spiritual journey if I work with their values and resources. There is a challenge of conflicting beliefs with clients and colleagues. I have seen many with fixed, rigid or even fundamentalist views. This seems to be getting better. For instance, I do not get the born-again types pushing their agenda on me so much now. Perhaps I am a "lost cause".

Regarding spirituality and organizations:
I have worked within a Christian organization, and felt the strong values, and the supportive and caring community. Fortunately, my employers affirmed the value of each person's spiritual journey or religious belief. They were careful about a clinical incorporation of spirituality into the care of clients but did seek to facilitate and encourage client's spiritual journey using a designated staff position.
I seek to help with meaning and purpose and find out what makes each individual. The *Strengths Model* I often use helps with identification of sustaining values.
If we are able to talk about perspectives, and behaviours in the face of illness. If that is "on the table", then I can promote to some degree the healing qualities of spiritual endeavours. Otherwise to whom will they really talk to, and who affirms them?

Thus, I do not have to provide answers, as I do not have them! Apart from my own belief system which I have available to share, (Such as in my other books). I do see a void often, but I cannot say "here do this/believe this".

I can try to ask questions that lead to these questions:

> *What is my purpose here?*
> *Who am I and what am I?*

I think the key to addressing spirituality in the caring professions is to create more opportunities such as inclusion in the training curriculum. (I am a clinical educator as per my post-grad qualifications and expertise). We need talking about it more often, as well as more formal learning avenues for staff. It needs to be "multi-faith", where religions are concerned and, I think, "multi-belief". (To make this dialogue respectful and safe). This could be tricky for someone to facilitate, whilst also holding a fixed religious belief.

> My "shopping list" therefore looks like this: *Inclusive language, less clinical terminology, no religion specific vocabulary, no ridicule. (E.g. saying Hindu idol worship is bad or even satanic). Promoting sacredness in all beings, and encounters. Maintain a focus on peace harmony and serenity. Healing spirituality as part of "treatment".*

My personal spirituality is a foundation for my own coping and satisfaction for life, and for my ability to facilitate healing. I want somehow to touch on the sacredness of life. The experience of spirituality transcends any language that I can use to describe it. I do try in this book!

Spirituality can be "meaning making" as opposed to an offshoot of traditional religion. The majority in the West now make clear statements that they are not religious, as in having a belief in a God or an afterlife. (Except for the U.S.A). Implications for physical and mental health are changing all the time let alone for those who want to be Pastors or Priests in a religion.

Yet more and more we see consistent reports that aspects of religious and spiritual involvement are associated with good health outcomes. In mental health, this seems more obvious if it means symptom reduction in disorders, due to a spiritual dimension or intervention

My questions, (answered and unanswered), that emerge from this entire topic concerning application of spiritual perspectives for professional are:

> *How does all this apply to mental health and alcohol and other drugs, (M.H. and A.O.D.), practitioners/professionals?*
> *What is the relationship between their religious and spiritual involvement and their professional and higher learning involvement?*
> *Where do these elements fit with these same people's academic and higher education journey?*
> *Where do all these elements fit with the organizations that are also undergoing significant changes in these areas?*

What I can answer is in the nature of a "shopping list" of what spirituality will do for our mental well-being, as a result of connectedness to a spiritual being or force.

Meaning of life, awe/wholeness/integration/Divine love/inner peace/serenity/harmony inner strength/hope/optimism. Kindness to others/selflessness/forgiveness. Anything I missed out?

My devotional/yogic/meditative practices seem to meld together my personality, (good and bad), and provide some sense of direction/order and dare I say it - sanity. The spiritual dimension does not exist in isolation from my work. Nor regarding family or other dimensions, even though I am sometimes keen to "get to my cave". It is integrative, not destructive. It is tied up with all my physical experience, feelings, thoughts and relationships.

For me, spirituality and religion have different meanings, but not different as in "on another planet". For me in fact often spirituality and religion sit side by side, but I accept that for many they have different meanings. My religion is a set of beliefs and practices, that has ancient historical roots, but my spirituality can also be categorized to some degree. Like this:

Being connected to everyone and everything in the Universe.

My Gurus say:
"We are not here by accident. We are spiritual creatures, and for each of us there is a plan and a purpose. Discovering that! Recognise the fundamental wholeness and interconnectedness of human beings, indeed the whole of *Life and the Universe*".

Spirituality and learning

In the quest for knowledge, eschew fundamentalism.

Strong moral beliefs are all well, but
intolerance to modern science and dogmatic
reactivity are "so yesterday".

Time to move on from the old rigid views of religion. Educational institutions can help by not imposing limits on what they teach as Religious Studies

You may call it spiritual or religious, but if it is dogmatic, intolerant, undemocratic and bigoted, it is doing more harm than good.

Best then to have no faith!

Spiritual centres are useful communities to societies, if they do not stifle unorthodoxy. Similarly, this is the case for therapeutic centres, such as those based on 12-step models. If it is fundamentalist, it is lost!

"The Truth shall set them free", but no one owns the Truth. Truth itself is free to anyone. The force of dogma will block the search for Truth.

We may live within a liberal democratic society. A society with a diversity of what could be incompatible perspectives on God, culture (and politics), functions well, and we are free to believe whatever religion/s we want to, legally. (Which means we have legal recourse if we are subject to discrimination based on our beliefs).

Dictatorship or Communism can decree how religion can be practiced, and some countries are Islamic States, seemingly curbing to some degree other beliefs. (Or even openly persecuting followers of some beliefs). I am lucky. I can be Multi Faith. It is my choice.

In Western countries, religion for many people can be "part of the picture". Religion then is no more than a part of life. Still, important, if that is the choice. A portion nonetheless for many and for many having little to do with their lives at all. (Politically, or more importantly morally).

In Islamic States, religion is anything but a part of life, as it shapes most aspects of the political and economic activity, and the culture of those societies. Beliefs though can then grate against other cultures views when it comes to law and punishment, and freedom in moral issues. (Often to do with sexual activity).

There are many religiously based institutions of education in most countries. It just that mostly they educate within certain religions and certain belief systems.

So, who is right? No one!

There are remnants of the past, which will eventually lose all meaning both against scientific standards and against future holistic views regarding spirituality.

We could say that the existence of religious belief is manifestation of vitality in society. Only if there is some opportunity for a Multi Faith perspective! (Alternatively, Multicultural)

Some are called to live out religious convictions. I was a "Hindu type" monk in India, but on moving back to the West adopted the norms around me.

So why still do religiously based institutions threaten academic freedom? Simple. When I was in India, I "toed the line". It was actually necessary to get my basic survival needs met. I did not see it that way at the time, and only after moving back to the West I saw that many in other religious group were under some pressure to conform.

It is probably not logically wrong for a group of people to get together to form a group grounded on one or another form of religion, nor for such a group to be a bit unwelcoming to those of other religion. Even if they think that another religion is "the work of Satan". Freedom of speech and thought is fundamental to our society, (even if bigotry is fairly common). It will take the future years to mature society to a point where dogmatism and fundamentalism goes "out of fashion".

Chapter 9
Practical Enlightenment

Surrender

There seems to be some idea that spiritual surrender is about giving up our attachments

This seems more like acceptance, where we accept life "as it is" Then, we sit in our Divine knowledge and whatever happens is Prarabdha. (A Sanskrit word for the accumulated force of past karma). This where a Brahma Gyani sits. (Knows themselves, as one with the Cosmic Soul, Brahman). Hence the word Gyana, which is knowledge of Brahman, the Cosmic Soul. The individual soul is called the Atman, and this topic is written about this when the ancient philosophy of Vedanta was discussed in "Om Divine Grace".

When you surrender spiritually, you stop making or seeking solutions to the uncontrollable. In the 12-step model its "my life became uncontrollable". (Hence then the need to surrender to a Higher Power). To stop seeking solutions also seems to be about acceptance. Surrender is willful acceptance and yielding to a dominating force and its will. Acceptance helps you accept the good and bad equally.

However, surrender also is to become aware of the Divine as oneself, with the Higher Power's energy *within*, and to accept it. It involves a shift in belief or approach to the spiritual journey, and is about "Who am I?"

Is this a catalyst for enlightenment?

Trust, and faith that there is a Divine Force seems to be a pre-requisite for surrender. "I believe that God will help me through this". This requires some awareness of options generated by the usual questioning that goes until a belief in the Divine co-exists with faith in your spiritual teachers.

Not just: What is this all about?

But also: What do I do (as service)?

The act of surrender requires some practical substance also. Mediation, prayer, chanting, using a mantra etc. What is the single most powerful tool you use on your spiritual journey? You can't think "I don't have to do anything else", and not do the practice required.

By turning your awareness away from normal activity and settling the mind, you can reconnect with your inner space. In the silent spaces beyond thoughts, you surrender to a Sound, the Cosmic Sound. Just as there is noise in life, there is noise in realization. It is very different though and can't be explained, only experienced.

You submerge your ego, which remains but is transformed, into identity as the Divine, where there is the bliss of Oneness. (When you can hear then the Cosmic Sound).

If all else fails, just pray for surrender. It doesn't matter who or what you pray to, it matters only that you are willing. The intention to surrender will allow its own release, and who knows, maybe there is an old man up there sitting in the clouds! (For me it's the Goddess, but I'm not saying my beliefs are any less "naïve")! Anything that helps with the letting go of fear and unending desire is worth a try.

Again, the small self, the individual "me," is not capable of dropping its own sense of ego, even though the Atman is intertwined with the Brahman. (Just as water is water, whether in a drop or in a sea). Maybe the "rock bottom" of the addict or a state of impasse, or "the darkest night", triggers some transcendence. It a pity that it may have to occur this way! A realization "I simply cannot do it, can't win, can't complete, can't change the situation". Something has to change, even if is occurring within a state of mental disorder. Someone will come to attend to you even if temporarily, involuntary, as when mental health becomes life threatening.

If however, you trust the Divine then the Divine Grace leads from darkness to light.

When we agree to participate in the process of surrender to our Higher Power or place our lives in the hands of God then we are met by the Divine Force.

The change occurs when there is willingness to access and seek the Truth.

This makes us available to be witnessed and to witness.

We can then stop hiding and leave the past shames and fears behind.

The Divine Self as the individual soul can then be healed by Divine Grace.

Maybe medication, therapy, rehabilitation, or other treatments will work.

Maybe

Or rather all the healing opportunities in the world may be helpful "to a point'. Maybe

The issue finally is about being at another level.

This is not just about praying to seek the god, the higher power, or ones deity.

It's about being in one's own Higher Power, being in the Divine Self and experiencing Divinity in human bodily form.

We have been claimed by a situation where we may live very fearful human lives, whilst at the same time seeking redemption, solutions to suffering within and without our personal lives.

There is a necessity, or a choice, or we are pushed to move "past the past". To release all of life in a higher way through the encounter with one's own Divine Self.

The rubbish or garbage is put out, and there is no need to check and go through it all. Just throw it out! Let it go to leave the darkness behind.

Freedom from self-condemnation, anger or righteous action, becomes grounded and light, and only then is the darkness absent.

Some would say that the material reality is an illusion.

The Sanskrit word for this is Maya, the delusional dreamlike transitory life experience.

The true Maya though is that we believe there is happiness all around us. In success, money, and even relationships.

The Buddha indicated that "all life is suffering"

Thus, life and free will at a high level seeks not to totally alleviate personal strife, but to see the Truth of life's journey as having an ultimate benefit for all. Cancer is not eliminated. Mental health disorders are not eliminated. Poverty is not eliminated. War is not eliminated.

We just don't participate from the same angle anymore; we have a radically different perspective and understanding of what is the universal Divine Consciousness.

Which cannot be in truth separate from anything or anyone.

Either this "consciousness" is homogeneous, or it

doesn't exist for a benefit, (as it would not then be anything of spiritual value)!

The ending of delusion, the end of the chase of dragons and dreams, can be celebrated.

Accomplished by agreeing and participating in the spiritual journey, and that can be accomplished by being on a path of one's personal choice.

There are signposts, teachers, and guides to help us. Even that the parts of religion that have not been corrupted can serve a purpose on this journey.

It's all available if we seek it, but more than that it will only work if we let it.

That is where the challenge of surrender lives!

Acceptance

The outcome of surrender is that there follows acceptance.

Our God, Higher Power or Divine has a plan with

exactly what we need to be given when we need.

This seems scary!

What if it's not true!

What if I don't like what I get?

It's a bit like going to a restaurant having to eat what is placed in front of oneself, instead of ordering.

What if I get non-vegan?

Or fish?

The good thing is that confusing choices can be released. What do I do about my marriage? What do I do about my job?

The Divine ensures that each step is revealed to one who makes the surrender and waits.

Answers come with surety as the inner voice, which only makes good sense, it's a true voice.

Thus, a word of warning. Those who are mental health professionals are well aware of the delusional content of the mind in states of sickness, when thoughts can be misleading, dangerous and life-threatening.

It may pay to check things out with a suitable professional person, guide, or therapist.

It's also a good idea to do so with a health professional if one is susceptible to unraveling, or is vulnerable to a mental health condition.

The issue is not really about what will happen to you, or what you will do, or how your five-year plan will work out. It's about sitting in a space where fear and anxiety about, *Life and the Universe* is alleviated.

Of course we desire, we want great things, and that lottery win.

Being in the Divine place is not about forceful relinquishing of our desires or even addictions.

It's about being in a space where it is natural to accept the fullness of life "as it is", and thus the needs and wants to disperse, vanish or become irrelevant.

Gratefulness for what we have not what we haven't got.

Acceptance is that there is enough, and I can share fully what I have got.

I don't have to win to the detriment of others. (Maybe sport is different).

Being one with the Divine Self will enable outcomes of benefit without or beyond limitation.

Far greater things can happen.

There still will be encounters in life that confuse, and cause fear and anxiety but again the Divine Design is that we learn.

Everything is included as part of the spiritual journey.

Thus, desire can be re-purposed and re-understood, as something to not fight against, but something that purposely placed in the correct position in the scheme of things.

Personal Enlightenment 1

Looking back some questions arise regarding my degree of spiritual attainment. Firstly, after having spent 10 years in India as a monk, and thirty plus years of struggling with mental health and addiction issues. Had I attained a state of self-knowledge and achieved Moksha? (Moksha is equivalent to Nirvana which is more common term in Buddhism. Moksha means freedom from the cycle of rebirth, or it just means freedom from this trouble human existence).

Release into what? Furthermore, had I found my own true religion and philosophy that can be substantiated, (somewhat), scientifically, and which can be now said to be lasting and permanent benefit all-round?

On leaving India I had developed a clearly defined Hindu derived Vedantic philosophical look on life which did not change with in the passage of time. This was not about having multiple gods, sitting in temples, but was about a very monotheistic outlook that was or even ultra-monotheistic possibly. I have written about Vedanta my previous book in some depth. I find the Vedanta philosophy enables a deeps sense of satisfaction. That I have something that is Truth Unlimited, which is unaffected or swayed by any or all religious type beliefs. It is about oneself as the Divine and about *Maya*, the illusory and transient suffering filled nature of "Life and the Universe". Vedanta though seemingly a nihilistic or fatalistic, has given me the means to develop calmness and equipoise, and helped alleviate the ups and downs of life.

Here are referred to an understanding, of philosophy statements, whereas realization of *"Aham Brahma Asmi"*, (I am the Cosmic Soul), is a completely different and more powerful awareness. This could be called enlightenment or realization. However, as previously written I have a problem with spiritual enlightenment and consider that true enlightenment occurs only on completion of the spiritual journey and all components of the worldly experience journey.

My own practice led me to a state where I had the opportunity and ability to control not only major elements of my own life but also that of others if I wished, through yogic powers called siddhis.

Somewhat strangely I had taken those "powers" from India into the everyday life of marriage, children, career, and found that my spiritual energy seem to have faded.

Then a feeling of being powerless over my human condition seemed to prevail for quite a few years. Although this was for a seemingly lengthy period, I believe it gave me eventually the "turbo charged realization", the ability to be realized at all levels of the mind/body, *whilst fully in the world.*

This is the state I call *Practical Enlightenment or Realistic Realization.*

My regained sense of control over circumstance, which is influence and self-regulated by my understanding of the workings of karma and prarabda, about which I write. This means a complex awareness of both the inevitability of some events and the endless possibility of change.

Ultimately total self-responsibility leads away from the known spiritual pathways and into the depths of Divine Grace!

A "Statement"

The Deity or God/Goddess is beyond description, but could be seen as the totality of all and thus is "perfect or complete". This creation and the creator are then: *Life and the Universe.*

This phenomenal world can then be seen as perfect for our requirements whether that is to enjoy, ("eat, drink and be merry"), or to do penance in caves, and return to out Divine state.

Incidentally we are already Divine, but are enveloped in the illusory powers of Maya, and thus think we are body/mind, personality and ego.

We are perfect and complete as we are.

Whatever is produced of the Cosmic Consciousness cannot be a duality of good and evil. Or enjoyment and pain cannot be different! (This is "advanced consciousness")!

The whole is complete in itself. But the universe emanates from Him, (or Her).

Everything must then be in complete balance. Even when that balance is chaos, pandemics, wars and planet loss.

(As happens apparently at the end of this era called Kali Yuga).

Everything animate or inanimate that is within the universe is controlled and owned by the one Deity.

This is because ones Deity varies. It can be inside of a religion or as a Higher Power or something else.

We all choose something different as per our culture, religion or belief system. We all possible differ even if slightly on an individual basis when it comes to our perception of, say, the Buddha or the Christ. (Even if we are in the same "subset", of Catholicism or Tibetan Buddhism etc.)

One should be happy therefore to accept only those things necessary for life, but of course we all want for ME.

We have a quota, as our lot in life, because we are sustained by life itself, which is of course Divine. Our delusion within consciousness identifies via our ego/personality with the external worlds and sees our wants and desires as of primary importance.

This then leads to the illusion of not having enough, not being good enough, and in its extremities may lead to self-harm and suicidal thoughts! Matter is impermanent, since it is created in birth and destroyed in death. The external world ages and changes. Your house will be gone in a thousand years! Probably.

This process, including death, or loss, usually gives rise to fear, and we want to "get stuff fast", as we don't understand the real issues nor ask the right questions.

Who am I?

What am I?

What is my real purpose?

The answers: My name. A human. To procreate

But are you just a name? Just a human? Just here to produce offspring?

If you're happy with that, throw this book away!

We usually don't know who we are. Because we don't pursue questions related to meaning and consciousness. We ignore them, for logical and very human reasons. Too scary!

We want to control nature also.

It's scary because we then have to confront the facts that all is just momentary, and pleasure, drugs, alcohol, sex are not a permanent solution to birth, old age, death and disease.

Surrender seems like loss of all, but acceptance allows for real freedom from fear. You find out who you really are and what the world really is.

The world has been here for a long, long time. Don't worry about it. Worry about your identity and the basic questions of existence: What is reality? What is experience? Who is experiencing? These spiritual questions can take you to a blissful alternative.

Whatever you do will garner learning

Culminating into knowledge, eventually.

Acceptance requires that you lose your ego/personality. Except the useful bits!

There is nothing like a suitable mantra, to "shortcut" the whole process.

Usually that means guidance, and possibly a living Guru.

We all are a collective and individual consciousness simultaneously. We are all seeking true pleasure.

We all are seeking the ultimate truth. We all are seeking immortality, an end to all misery/nothingness.

Mantra - it is a combination of special sounds and vibrations that purify space, body, mind and consciousness from negative energies. Mantra – it is an ancient sacred formula that gives a powerful Divine energy, and it is the key that opens the way to the Supreme Divine knowledge. Repeat the mantras as much as possible.

A Rosary also helps with concentration on the mantra and meanings, for the beginner.

Again get advice on this from somewhere (The Internet is better than nothing)!

Epilogue

However, time moves on and hopefully this service through teaching will move through a spiritual growth.

Growth means our identities change, and especially if we move to a more focused life.

I outgrew what I had in India, and I actually became bored sitting as a monk in my little hut in the middle of nowhere.

Then I had no watch, no newspapers, no radio, no running water or electricity.

That wasn't a problem, as it seems that we adapt quite easily when the issue is about spiritual identity.

Since then, I've had the trajectory of marriage, children, and career.

I still have my professional practicing certificate,

driving license and bank account!

In my so-called human identity, I am similarly somewhat bored with the incessant noise of so-called civilization around me.

True: I am competent, functional and relate to people in a caring and friendly manner.

Definite definitely time to move on!

But to what though?

I'm not going off anywhere, and certainly not to live in a cave.

I don't have the money to buy a small Greek island, cruise around the world, or do some other things requiring major wealth.

I guess regarding being in my spiritual "place of residence" it comes down to this:

Who am I?

What am I?

What is my role in life now?

With this availability to take on a fresh adventure, or place in life, comes willingness to take on any new given named identity.

I have surrendered to my Goddess.

The wait is based on being expectant and ready to move into whatever is directed.

Writing is one of the new roles.

Being a writer of the spiritual journey.

Another is, to be available, in this role.

To help others in their spiritual journey

Having a more counselling/therapist focus in my professional work.

We all get ideas or feelings sometimes about the way things are going to go.

Life becomes an adventure when there is surrender. That is if we are focused on meditation or mantras, and are able to access our inner souls and selves

When the choice of "how to be' is made then there is a whole different pathway opening up.

In a sense this is the final pathway, as a knowing of

the Truth pathway is about being where one is in the moment, and then the journey ceases, as there is nowhere then to go! Whilst still having the openness and awareness of the needs of one day at a time. It's a game where one is directed to serve and yet see the illusion inherent in all experience.

If the service itself is the meaning of life, then it's not about oneself or the ego driven selfish personality. There is no spiritual path happening if whatever one is doing is not about others.

Even just Being comes into this category, as there is no point doing it as an exercise in feeling good or packing in the bliss, if it's just about me.

So here is the prayer.

That the Goddess be directly involved in leading into the next phase, the next opportunity, and the next identity. I release my control and expectation. I surrender to the given plan for my service.

Hari Om Tat Sat.

About Raymond
In my younger years, from 1976, I was a monk in India for 10 years. (*Ganesh Giri Paramhansa*). *I write & talk about Yoga, Mantras, Kundalini, and Gurus.* I have been a Mental Health Practitioner since 1980.

https://www.amazon.com/author/om-divine-grace-mantra-yoga

My web/blog site: www.goddessmantra.guru

Also, Om Divine Grace podcasts/ Mantra Guru-Raymond YouTube – for Kundalini tutorials.
My books are in paperback & eBooks:

English-Man, Beggar-Man, Holy-Man

My journey overland to India in 1976, & my 10 years there a monk

Divine Grace Journey

The post-India years spiritual journey plus teachings

The Transcendental Guru by Paramhansa Ganesh Giri

On Divine Grace Yoga by Paramhansa Ganesh Giri

Therapeutic Journeys to Self-Realisation

MY MANTRA ART:
https://fineartamerica.com/art/raymond+pattison

Mantra for Enlightenment from:
mantraguru.raymond@gmail.com